THE
FOOD
TRAVELER'S
HANDBOOK

*How to find cheap, safe and delicious food
anywhere in the world.*

Jodi Ettenberg

The Food Traveler's Handbook: How to find cheap, safe and delicious food anywhere in the world.

ISBN 978-0-9877061-6-4

ISBN 978-0-9877061-6-4

Cataloguing data available from Library and Archives Canada

Disclaimer:

This book provides entertaining and informative snapshots of the writer's personal experiences and helpful tips from the writer and others, learned while traveling and eating around the world. The tips provided in this book are not meant to serve as an exclusive checklist to effectively safeguard the reader in every travel situation. Each reader should complete updated, detailed research from legitimate sources to learn the cultural norms and safety recommendations for their specific destination. No one can guarantee safety and travel can expose everyone to potential risks. Because safety is impacted by each person's actions and choices, readers are advised to always do their homework on their destination and use their best judgment while on their journey.

I wish you safe, happy and delicious travels.

For Joel S.,
who taught me that even the simplest of foods
have a story of their own.

Acknowledgements

Many people from far-flung places around the globe contributed to make this book a reality.

Sarah Button, thank you for reviewing the book in its initial stage and for editing it with comments that included Star Wars references. Cheryl and Brian, Bessie and Kyle, Nadia and Mathieu, thank you for temporary housing and copious hugs; Shira and Matt, thank you for emergency printing runs. I am indebted to the people who helped me improve the numerous drafts of this book, as well as those who have provided their reviews: Tyler Cowen, Naomi Duguid, Janice Waugh, Shannon O'Donnell, James Clark, Mike Sowden, Ana Botelho, Mike Rigney, Tracey Nesbitt, C.C. Chapman, Spud Hilton, Cameron Stauch, Sarah and Terry Lee, Jeff Jung and the members of the JAIL Google group. Your thoughtful but firm feedback was much appreciated. Thank you Pam Mandel and Eugene Buchko for your grammar fixes. To the many food-obsessed writers, cooks and travelers who contributed quotes to this handbook, many thanks. The book is much more valuable with your advice.

To all four of my parents, my brother Cale and my stepsister Jen and her husband Jon, I'm thankful for a good number of things, but specifically that you let me write this book in a corner, despite the fact that you hadn't seen me in months.

Finally, a big thank you to the readers of *Legal Nomads* who emailed to ask for food advice and share their travel stories, and who inspired me to write this book.

Contents

Contents

Contents

My Unexpected Love Affair with Food

I grew up in a household that wasn't very focused on food. Mealtimes were a chance to sit and talk about our days, and often about the politics of the places we wanted to visit. My mother's educational background was in history and she would regale us with stories from around the world, turning our dinner times in Montreal into a fabulous soap opera spanning centuries. But the food itself was an afterthought, an accessory to the discussion. There were no spicy dishes and little emphasis on international flavors. Though eating and history were intertwined in my childhood, it took two decades before I began to learn about them together.

In the intervening years, when I worked as a lawyer in New York, I took vacations like everyone else. I set out on short trips to China and France and elsewhere with a list of sights to see, but returned home with vivid memories of the foods I had tried and the markets I had explored. Food gradually became the theme that linked my travels. When I returned to my job in New York, I began to choose my meals more carefully, exploring the city as I had explored others: to find the tastes and stories that inspired instead of those that merely filled my stomach.

By the time I quit my job as a lawyer to travel full-time in April 2008, my curiosity about food had turned into a quest. I realized that I could eat to survive, or I could use my food choices as a springboard to deeper knowledge about the places I visited, asking questions, befriending locals, and trying to truly understand how people ate, and why. While it took me several years to start writing about it, those who traveled with me saw firsthand that my days were planned almost entirely around food.

The tipping point in my realization that gastronomy was at the core of my passions occurred while daydreaming after a dinner in Thailand, full from a fiery green curry and coconut soup. In a post-meal glow, I mused aloud about what to eat for breakfast. Chicken porridge, or noodle soup? Did I want to head to the food cart under the expressway near my apartment and eat with the motorcycle taxi drivers on my street, or did I want to go to a local eatery under the SkyTrain and slurp up thick rice noodles and tender chicken topped with curled, fried garlic. So many choices, only one breakfast.

My dinner companion laughed, "We just ate! Are you always thinking about food?"

I glanced across the table. "Well, yes," I said with a smile. "Aren't you?"

The answer, of course, was a resounding "no." Somehow, along the way, I had turned my quest for learning by traveling into a quest to learn through food. Without a doubt, my thoughts drift inevitably, inexorably toward my stomach.

Food, mostly cheap food, became the way that I wanted to see a country, to understand how it moved and why people did what they did. I found food to be the most effective way to get a glimpse of the soul behind the façade. Street food was the common denominator during most of my travels, the practical option available to everyone, tourists and locals alike.

I've wolfed down tacos al pastor in a suit in Mexico City along with men from nearby office buildings, their ties flung over their shoulders and their faces smeared with grease. Next to them, a taxi driver laughed at my obvious enjoyment of a local dish and murmured that I was eating as Mexicans do. I might have been there for a business meeting but I wasn't about to let my attire keep me from the street eats.

I've stuffed my knees under a wobbly table on the streets of Yangon, Myanmar, slurping down a breakfast of mohinga (fish noodle soup) with people from all walks of life on their way to work, their lips curled into a smile as they watched me try to eat without dropping all of the noodles back into the bowl. Of course, half of the broth ended up on my shirt.

These experiences are etched in my brain because they were not just about the food; they were about the connection to the place and its people that was forged in the process of eating. Food was the ultimate equalizer, both a need and an art form, regardless of how informally it was served.

Many of those impromptu street meals turned into conversations, often with enthusiastic hand gestures, and then an invitation to eat in someone's home. Frequently these invitations stemmed from my appreciation of the food I was eating. Complimentary words from me led to a response in the form of a challenge: "Oh, you think this is good food? You should try my cooking instead." A casual shopping excursion for spices in Meknes, Morocco led to a discussion with a woman about which of the spice blends was best for cooking inside traditional clay tagines, and then an effusive invite to dine at her house later that week.

There is no secret to forging these connections with others, though there are various tips in this handbook to facilitate them. All you need is an adventurous set of taste buds, a mind open to connecting and learning from others and, of course, a good appetite. There is great food to be had anywhere if you know where to look, and my go-to places remain the markets and the streets. Sitting at a table, listening to hissing oil and street vendors yelling over the din of their customers - this is what makes me smile.

In my travels, I've also had the wonderful opportunity to frame greater philosophical discussions around my mealtimes, learning as I ate and building my understanding of how the puzzle pieces of the modern world fit together. Food is universal, and we are all able to build bridges between our cultures through what we choose to eat. A sense of adventure and a myriad of tastes converge when I arrive somewhere and head straight to the markets, and it is unmistakably joyous.

From a childhood with no spices and very little international food, my travels catapulted me into a world of people and places connected through history and an intersection of flavors. I learned how to prepare tagines and rich curries, crispy pork and noodles, and through it all, I picked up many tips for safe eating along the way.

Mutton tagine from a roadside stall in Zaita, Morocco.

Why the Emphasis on Cheaper Eats?

The tips in this book, and the stories that accompany them, focus on cheaper, local fare. Like many travelers, I enjoy a fine dining experience and genuinely admire the chefs and artisans who use creative techniques to bring food to a new level.

When exploring the world, however, many of the friendships I've made have begun in eateries that people frequent on a day-to-day basis – the markets, the carts at the side of the road, the rickety tables that provide a cramped but incomparably authentic eating experience. Those are the meals I have focused on here.

There is a fallacy in North America and parts of Europe that cheaper food is not quality cuisine, something reinforced by an abundance of processed food choices. In much of the world a roadside meal is not only the freshest and tastiest option but also an ideal way to discover the building blocks of what a society eats, and why. Moreover, it serves as an entry point to a rabbit hole of conversations, one topic leading to the next, all ignited by a common desire to enjoy food.

❝ *To me, eating cheaply is not a matter of expense; it's a matter of hanging out with the coolest people, and eating the most bad-ass food! Whenever I look for the soul of a city, I look for what the workers eat every day. I look for what's common in the greasy spoons and where it's the best, and I look for what the people go boggles over late at night -- that's the real stuff. And it's usually cheap.* **❞**

Jeff Orlick
Urban food explorer and creator of iwantmorefood.com

Watching and Learning from a Tiny Plastic Chair

Focusing on street stalls affords a unique vantage point to observe the nature of a place and its people. The practice for many vendors is to use furniture that would otherwise seem at home in a kindergarten classroom: a tiny table with matching chairs. Part of the street food experience often includes folding my body to fit under these furnishings, crouching down knees to chin. The advantage of these plastic tables and chairs is that they offer a sightseeing venue of their own. Yes, there is the benefit of spending less for fresh food. Yes, I can connect with locals on a different level. But even if I am not asking questions, I am watching. While eating my soup at a crowded street stall, I can look around and see the patterns and pleasures of those around me.

On any given day, busy street vendors split their time among their dining tables, the many motorcycles piled high with people waiting for a meal to go, and those who wander up to pick up some food to consume at home. The dance between groups of people seeking a meal takes place against a backdrop of dining. While a motorcycle skids up to the stall to procure a dish for take-away, a family is also sitting and sharing dinner. One, two or three kids at a table - and usually a grandparent too - sit in the calm eye of the hurricane, surrounded by the chaos of food noise. Though you aren't at an established tourist venue, you are provided with an unfiltered, nuanced snapshot of an evening or morning in the life of locals.

In contrast, restaurants catering to tourists do not afford the opportunity to absorb a city's atmosphere while you eat. They might offer authentic and delicious local fare, but the environment is different. In cultures where street food abounds, those tourist restaurants rarely supply you with learning layers over and above the food. The confluence of people, smells and tastes that you are privy to merely by eating on the street is very special. And it is not something that can be replicated indoors.

If food is a lens through which to see the world, a seat at one of those tiny tables offers the best view.

Young girl at a food stall in Vientiane, Laos.

Where Restaurants Come in Handy

That is not to say that you should ignore restaurants entirely. Variety is important and often comparing a street food iteration of a dish you love with one from a nearby restaurant is an excellent way to assess your taste buds. Can you taste the price difference in that plate of fried rice? I have found that the street stall version tends to taste better, but it was a fun game to play on my travels, testing each to see how they matched up.

Eating on the street is also a good marker for restaurant pricing. Once you know the customary price for a street meal, sourcing that same dish at a restaurant tells you how much they are charging for their service and environment. For example, after eating my share of *nasi goreng* (fried rice) at markets during my 2009 visit to Bali, Indonesia, I knew that the average price was 5,000 – 6,000 Rupiah. As a result, I tried to stick to restaurants that offered the same plate for 11,000 Rupiah or less. Anything more and I would be stepping into a place that clearly catered to tourists and not locals.

While not fail-safe, testing out food markets - like I did with my *'nasi goreng test'* - is an excellent way to make your eating choices more informed.

The Exceptions to the Cheap Eats Rule

While I am biased toward street stalls as first fronts of learning, there are certainly countries where some of the best meals are not found roadside. This occurs in two main cases:

- when the street food culture is not as prevalent for the general population (that is, where only a certain group of people tends to eat on the street, such as taxi or bus drivers), or
- when the best food is particularly complicated to prepare, meriting a sit-down event.

Dinnertime street meals are the norm in Thailand, with people stopping at the food stalls on their way home from work. On the other hand, in Jordan the general population may grab *shawarma* or *falafel* on the go, but at dinnertime you won't find masses of locals sitting out on the street to eat. Therefore, some of the more mouth watering and historically interesting dishes in Jordan – *mansaf* (lamb cooked in dried yogurt and served with rice or bulgur) or *zerb* (meat baked on a grill in a hole in the ground, traditionally a Bedouin dish) – are best consumed at a restaurant. You won't even see versions of those dishes on the street; they take too long to make, and are not scalable for quick roadside eating.

Similarly, visitors to Morocco might think at first glance that the locals only consume tagines and grilled skewers. Street stalls tend to focus on those dishes, targeting the many truck, bus and taxi drivers that ply the dusty roads. But Morocco's history is flush with a wide array of other dishes: seafood, saffron-infused rice and even a sweet and nutty pigeon version of an empanada called *pastilla*. You would miss those dishes if you stuck only to the street food.

How do you know when to eat on the street and when to try a restaurant? One option is to track down the national dish and see how involved the preparation is. Wikipedia lists national dishes by country (en.wikipedia.org/wiki/National_dish), which provides a framework for discovering what foods a place is known for. Another option is to see what the locals do for breakfasts and dinners. Are they eating in food courts or markets? In countries where you see people eating at home for the most part, you will find restaurants a good supplement to the street options. The places celebrated for their street foods – Bangkok, Singapore, Hong Kong – all have an established culture of eating at hawker stalls as a matter of course.

Bedouin woman kneading *jameed*, a dried yoghurt used in *mansaf* and other Jordanian dishes.

A Primer on Hawker Stalls

Hawker stalls are groups of food stalls primarily in Singapore (though also found in Hong Kong, Malaysia and Indonesia). Eating is one of the great pleasures in Singapore, and the island had street cart vendors who would roam the roads with their mobile kitchens. Eventually, the government subsidized rents for central parts of the city where some of the carts could park on a semi-permanent basis, allowing for more control over cleanliness and hygiene. As a result, there are some terrific clusters of food courts at malls, intersections and office buildings in Singapore that are a safe bet for tasty, fresh meals. When people refer to hawker stalls, they are referencing these constellations of food vendors. Singapore's diverse cultures share a passion for food and the hawker stalls are an ideal place to watch that enthusiasm in action.

Who Is this Handbook For?

The twin storylines of history and spices have molded the way I see the world and have channeled my travels toward eating as much as possible. Readers of my travel blog, *Legal Nomads*, have reached out, asking how they can do the same. They have shared concerns about getting sick and about being overwhelmed by the staggering assortment of choices, yet they were united in their desire to learn through food.

It was a natural step, then, to write this handbook on how to eat cheaply and safely around the world. Over the years, I have used food as the lens through which I learn about a place: as a way to connect to locals, understand their traditions and culture, and keep myself on a path of discovery.

In addition to putting together tips from my own travels, I've reached out to experts on several continents – chefs, bloggers, writers and other food-obsessed travelers. I have included some of the fun cultural quirks that make eating so fascinating. This book provides a framework for experiencing the world a little differently, using all of your senses - especially sight and taste.

It is not only the long-term traveler who can use food as the primary tool for understanding the spirit of a place. Observing how and what people eat can be a conduit for learning on shorter trips or weekend getaways too.

Adventures abound when you base your learning around something as basic – and universal – as food.

66 *Food delights us, food unites us, food embodies the soil, the sea and the weather, the farmer's sweat and the fisherman's toil. But as these tales and my own edible adventures reveal, food is only part of the feast. Every meal, whether a single mango or a multicourse molecular masterpiece, is really a communing of spirit: just as important are the setting and the situation, the effort, attentiveness and intention that infuse and inform what we share. We feast on the love behind and within the offering, love for a moment, a lesson, a gift, for companions and connections, that will never be repeated and can never be replaced.* **99**

Don George
A Moveable Feast at Page 10

A perfect breakfast of chicken noodle soup in Luang Prabang, Laos.

Jodi Ettenberg

DISCOVERING
THE WORLD
THROUGH
FOOD

Roadside Tapas in Luang Prabang, Laos

On my last day in Luang Prabang, Laos I met a young chef from Australia as I wandered once again through the morning food markets. It was the fourth time that I had found myself in the market's maze of soups and leathery water buffalo jerky, its piles of tiny, bright purple eggplants spread out on blankets with the weary women who sold them. He caught me staring at a particularly lovely eggplant arrangement and struck up a conversation; it became apparent rather quickly that we were both obsessed with food. We spent the rest of the afternoon enthusiastically talking about where our respective travels had taken us.

Because it was my last evening in town, I had arranged to meet fellow travelers for dinner in a narrow alleyway off the night market. The alley boasted many all-you-can-eat noodle and vegetable buffet stalls and fish grilled over coals, but I never saw locals eating there, despite its proximity to a main thoroughfare. I had invited the chef for dinner and on the walk over, we spied a series of motorcycles slowing down to pick up food for the night, one street away from the market. While there was nowhere to sit, there were dishes aplenty, stacked high in metal trays at the edge of the street. I headed over for a closer look, finding a slew of dips and sauces, red tomato stews and smoky eggplant (so that is where all the eggplant went!), all served with a side of sticky rice in a clear plastic bag. A tiny grill held fatty cuts of pork, brushed with chili oil and tied to pieces of bamboo with twine.

The Australian chef and I exchanged a look, turned to watch more Laotians skid to a stop and point at one, two, three of the dips and make off with rice. Without speaking, we knew we'd be ditching the buffet for something a little different. Watching the speed of the food turnover, we suspected it would be fresh, and with so many people stopping on the way home to pick up dinner for their families, surely it tasted good too?

We walked to the stall, cooing over the heaped plates of stewed meats and vegetables, buying tiny bags of them all, an instant Laotian version of tapas. Of course, we included sticky rice too. We found a tiny bamboo mat on the side of the market and sat cross-legged, spreading out our feast on pieces of banana leaves and scooping out the dips with hands full of rice. Our faces messy with red chili and tomato dip, fingers covered in eggplant and sticky with rice, with rivulets of spice-induced sweat beginning to spiral down our temples, we must have made quite a scene.

Within moments, several tuk-tuk drivers came over, hands clasped behind their backs, their curiosity evident. Shifting from foot to foot, they peered unabashedly at our makeshift dinner. Once they caught a glimpse of the moveable feast, they clapped their hands together and smiled, calling over more friends. "You *falang* (foreigners) like food from Laos!" Ten minutes later, we were in the center of a group of Laotians, who were happy we weren't eating baguettes and buffets like the rest of the tourists in town. Meal invitations followed, we asked questions about what ingredients went into the dips and many, many thumbs-up were given.

The lesson: even a small deviation from a travel routine reaps new tastes, memories and rewards.

Spicy *Jeow Mak Keua*, an eggplant dip from Laos.

Why Focus on Food When You Travel?

When I travel to a new place, I often make checklists of sights to see and places to stop and visit along the way. I want to understand what makes the country I'm visiting different, be it through the history of its buildings or UNESCO sites, or through the beauty of its landscapes. Examining a country through its food is another angle of understanding, an all-encompassing snapshot of what a place has to offer. In fact, I would argue that it is the most compelling tool we can use as travelers to discover the wonder of a new country or region.

Food hasn't caused me to ignore my checklists or the more established sights in a country – I just save them for later. My first option for discovering the culture and history of a place is now eating and observation, filling in the gaps that guidebooks and history books cannot capture with ease. The ancillary benefits to focusing on my plate have been as important as the taste of the food itself: observing the rhythms of mealtimes and the constrained chaos involved in preparing and enjoying food.

Instead of seeing eating as a necessity, I encourage you to view it as a lesson in creativity, the same way that you would approach planning the other elements of your trip.

But it is not just about learning. There are other compelling reasons to eat your way around the world instead of just visiting it.

The Art of Food Presentation

In a world of easily accessible photography and photo sharing, capturing the visual element of food has become a lasting way to record your feelings about a new place. Supermarkets, food stalls and even corner fruit shops are a feast for the eyes, allowing you to compare what you know against what you are discovering.

Many countries also focus on the visual in presenting their meals. In Japan, for example, the supermarkets sell food in delicate bento boxes, carefully prepared and perfectly stacked. *Kaiseki*, a multi-course traditional Japanese dinner, is a lesson in pristine presentation and elegant form – there is much to see and admire before you even pick up your chopsticks to eat. The emphasis on appearance dovetails with other concepts in Japanese culture, such as wabi-sabi (the art of finding beauty in imperfection) and minimalism.

In contrast, roadside tagine stops along Morocco's N9 roadway offer symmetrical, conical clay pots bubbling against a backdrop of the High Atlas Mountains. Presentation is not the focus, but it remains the primary takeaway. The value of these clay pots lies in their visual beauty and versatility. There is a large Moroccan population in Montreal, and while I was familiar with the tagine as a result, nothing prepared me for the sight of dozens of ochre cones at the side of the road, steam rising toward the heavens.

Hand-painted tagines from Fes, Morocco.

Spices Are Perfect Food Souvenirs

Food as a souvenir is nothing new. Growing up in Montreal, a friend from Italy would entertain me with stories of her grandfather's misadventures in trying to sneak home some Parma ham from a visit to Bologna, or her uncle stuffing fresh burrata cheese from Florence into his suitcase, inside an elaborate contraption of ice and plastic, for illicit consumption at home. While I don't advocate those kinds of extremes, often a food-based souvenir is an ideal gift for yourself or for those you love. Using it at home instantly transports you back to the smells, the tastes, and the feelings of discovery you experienced when you first tried it abroad.

Fresh chili peppers.

Compiling Recipes to Recreate at Home

Recipes are also perfect travel mementos, one of the best ways to bring back the food-filled enjoyment of a time away.

One of my favorite things to do when I arrive in a new place is to find a dish that I love and then search out a friendly street stall that offers it to the masses. I familiarize myself with the dish first, then circle back to my target and offer a service swap of sorts. I tell the vendor that I will bring guests from my hostel or hotel to the hawker stand for meals in exchange for being taught how to make a specific dish on the menu.

While some street vendors have balked at this idea, most have broken into a huge smile. Many vendors specialize in one main dish (or two or three), and build reputations around those simple options. By offering customers in exchange for recipes, I figured out a way to eat well and learn in the process.

I have engaged in this exchange in many countries around the world, with recipes to try upon my return visits to Montreal. It enabled me to not only connect to the vendors, who are mystified but flattered that I would take such an interest in their food, but also to see the conditions of their work environment as I stood many times over, watching them cook in the heat and humidity, and even (in Kuala Lumpur) in the monsoon rains.

The recipes I have accumulated from this experiment are not always mainstream, nor are they necessarily well-known variations on a popular dish. They are merely the expert offerings of particular families or cooks, and dishes that piqued my fancy as I traveled. In recreating them at home, I've brought friends and family along for the ride and provided them with new taste discoveries.

Foods Connect People Around the World

Food is a necessity, but also an instrument to pass cultural traditions and religious ceremonies down to subsequent generations. It forms a connective tissue among people of the same home, within a community and between travelers and the places they visit. Asking about the details of a particular dish or where to find an ingredient popular in a new town breaks the ice, and it creates common ground between strangers from far flung places. You will be amazed at the hospitality others will offer merely because you have taken a genuine interest in what is on their plates.

I will provide more practical tips about how to make those connections and source local eats below. However, it is worth mentioning that one of the reasons that food is so important is its unfailing ability to unite people from around the world.

Learning to Appreciate Hot, Spicy Meals

Our food tastes are formed by the flavors we grow up consuming. Although many towns have a broad international restaurant scene, providing us with exposure to foods from Ethiopia or Mexico or Thailand, even those of us who are more adventurous eaters have palates more accustomed to the foods in our own backyards. Thus, when we travel to places like Sichuan in China or taste our first som tam spicy papaya salad in Thailand, our taste buds are stunned. It's wonderful.

The first time I traveled to Asia was in 2004. I was taking a much-needed break following the conclusion of a long corporate deal. I took all of my vacation days at once and met a friend in China, looping from Hong Kong to Nanning, to Chengdu and back again to Hong Kong on my return flight. I had eaten Chinese food in Montreal, but it was nothing like eating it in China. For starters, I quickly learned that each province had its own regional cuisine, as disparate in style and taste as I could possibly imagine. And then there were my culinary adventures in Sichuan, home to the fiery, numbing Sichuan peppercorn. There, dishes took on a heat of their own; I remember ordering a grilled fish and watching in shock as it arrived, almost entirely covered in spicy chili peppers with only its eye visible through the carpet of red.

Sichuan pepper, I later discovered, is not actually a pepper at all but a red-brown dried berry of the prickly ash tree. Eating Sichuan peppercorns is a strange experience: it feels as though your taste buds have been possessed. It numbs your tongue and lips, and you can faintly register only a mottled mixture of fire, lemon and spice. As scientist Raven Hanna once noted: "There's a war in my mouth."[1]

The trip was not only an awakening for my taste buds, but also for a new understanding of just how different cultures of eating can be. What I thought was "tears pouring down my face" spicy was merely flavor to many of the Chinese people I met; when I ate my breakfast rice porridge with no extra chili oil, I was asked why I liked my food to taste like nothing. Of course, to me, it tasted great.

During my time in Thailand I watched locals pick up a fresh dish from a street stall, only to add additional tastes – chili, fish sauce with hot peppers, sugar, and often lime. I was confused; the dish seemed to be perfectly acceptable, so why add the extra garnish? But to Thais sitting nearby, my lack of post-cooking doctoring seemed out of place in a culture that expects its dishes to balance out among hot, sour, salty and sweet. They would pile spoonfuls of additional spice and sugar onto their shared plates, their taste buds seeking a flavorful symmetry that I did not yet know how to find.

Over time, I started adding more sugar, fish sauce and chilies to my own food, trying to do as Thais do. But to this day, I am unable to consume any dish "Thai spicy" – it is just too much.

A street meal in Chiang Mai, Thailand: grilled chicken, spicy green papaya salad and hot and sour coconut chicken soup.

Changing Your Taste Buds Over Time

Many of us have likely crossed paths with travelers outside their comfort zones when it comes to food. Instead of seeing food as a source of learning, they prefer to settle for the familiar, perhaps wondering why they cannot find a decent burger in town. One surefire way to defuse any hostility toward local foods is to invite those travelers to join you for dinner, all the while explaining where the dishes come from and how the basic local ingredients are transformed into such a flavorful meal.

As in China, Thailand's foods vary by regional custom. There is the sticky rice and the sweet-sour, spicy salads of the northeast, often served with grilled fish or meat; the coconut curries of the south; and in between, central Thai foods, often cooked in a wok and served with rice. You can disarm the traveler who says "I don't like Thai food" with an organized meal, taking the time to experiment not just with one dish but with the whole dining experience.

The approach described above also works well with families. Take the case of Ana, an 11-year-old girl from Florida who traveled to Asia for the first time in late 2011. By her own admission, she had no desire to eat the foods in the region, and flat-out refused to try them when she arrived. But bit by bit, she found the culture of eating intriguing: the fact that some meals required chopsticks and others a spoon and fork, the way Thais shared all of their plates on a table, the bags and bags of curries that people in Southeast Asia would take to-go on their commute home from work. Eventually, she started trying more of the foods and by the end of her six months in Asia, she was already feeling nostalgic for the tastes and traditions she would miss.

❝ *For other kids who are traveling and haven't ever tried any other foods before, I would say try everything. I mean it - try everything! You just have to go out of the familiar and be as adventurous as you can get, because that will get you the farthest when you travel, both comfort-wise and food-wise. I feel like you should at least try everything a couple of times because if you only try something new once, you're not going to like it because you've never had it before. So try it a few times before judging it. In the end, if you're a kid and all you've ever eaten is food from McDonalds, then you should definitely make it a point to try as many things as possible so you can see for yourself that food in other places is also very good.* **❞**

Ana
alittleadriftjr.com

Ana eating at a *chapatti* stand in Mandalay, Myanmar.

A Crash Course in Spicing Foods

I discovered spices in 2002, when I was living in the South of France. Not content with the fresh produce in my temporary home of Aix-en-Provence, I was drawn to the brightly colored spices piled high and sold in a corner of the market. With spices not figuring prominently in my childhood cuisine, the pungent smells fascinated me. The man who sold the spices was Moroccan, and he watched me quietly for days as I picked up my daily fruit. I always drifted by his stall, closing my eyes to take in the smells.

After a week, he finally broke his silence.

"You're never going to buy anything, are you?"

It caught me off guard; I could only laugh and shrug my shoulders sheepishly. "I'm living in university dorms – I don't even have a kitchen!"

But I needed to understand why those spices smelled the way they did and what they were used for. And I offered up a trade: I would teach him English to use with the tourists in town, if he would teach me about spices.

A routine developed during my months in France. On the days without morning classes, I would swing by the market for a crash course in cumin. I would skip Economic Integration Law to learn about tagine and the complicated thread of flavors that make it the beautiful dish that it is – one spice changed, one ingredient moved around and the overall taste shifted perceptibly in response. His stall was an intricate assortment of cinnamon and turmeric, saffron and paprika, and the crème de la crème, the spice blend of Ras-el-hanout. My hands and nostrils were full. Ras-el-hanout was particularly mystifying: made from a mix of dozens of spices, up to 30 or more in some cases, the complicated subtleties of the blend were a point of pride for spice vendors. This was a far cry from my usual, casual salt and pepper dusting. This was a whole new world.

I returned to Montreal harboring a deep appreciation for the building blocks of food and the spices that could be used to create something completely new. It is no surprise that I also returned home from my time abroad with a suitcase full of fragrant souvenirs: bags of fresh spices, stalks of dried plants, and, of course, an "herbes de Provence" dispenser. A tiny yellow cylinder filled with dried green leaves, it was full of the first herbs that I had tried during my sojourn in France. Every time I used some of the herbs I was transported back to those months of eating and discovery.

Colorful peppercorns from a spice market in Turkey.

Getting Over the Fear

Local Cheap Eateries Are Not as Scary as They Seem

Whether you are at home or abroad, preventing food poisoning altogether is impossible. The reality is that we aren't immune to food-borne illnesses in the West – there are instances of bacterial outbreaks in food here too. But the fear we face in trying new foods abroad is amplified by the fact that we are somewhere new, unaware of how food is supposed to be eaten, and unfamiliar with our surroundings. And, of course, we are worried that if we *do* fall ill, we won't be able to get proper treatment.

Getting past that fear of illness is worthwhile, but it does take a leap of faith. In presenting tips and tricks from years of travel, combined with suggestions from food writers, chefs and long-term adventurers, I hope that you will be ready to take the plunge, far into the (delicious) unknown. This book exists in part to help you avoid the pitfalls of unsanitary preparations in the search for good food.

By preparing ahead of time – with proper medication in case you do get ill, by learning about how food is treated in the places you visit, and by assessing street stalls to ascertain whether they are safe or not – you will gain confidence in eating as locals do. In addition, you will make connections and forge friendships in the process, which will certainly motivate you to return to that unsteady table where you ate breakfast the day before.

Despite dining more frequently on the street, I've fallen ill on more occasions eating at restaurants than from consuming street food. However, there were two circumstances when I did get food poisoning from street food, and in both of those cases I completely ignored the safety advice in this handbook.

In the first situation, the food was not cooked all the way through, but I was hungry and I ignored the warning bells in my head. (It was a llama empanada. With llamas being one of my favorite animals, friends have floated the theory of karmic retribution.) In the second situation, I saw the vendor washing out someone else's bowl with what looked to be river water - a river that I knew was not very clean. When I received my bowl of soup, I ate it, despite knowing the contents were likely contaminated.

I use these examples to illustrate that while it is impossible to completely prevent getting sick from food, safety precautions are a good start to putting your mind at ease.

Dietary Restrictions Can Be Addressed Safely

Another understandable concern is related to dietary restrictions, be they allergies, religious constraints, or pure choice. It can be daunting to travel knowing that there are certain foods or ingredients you need to avoid.

In tandem with discovering food as a conduit for learning, I was diagnosed with celiac disease, an autoimmune disease triggered by eating gluten found in wheat, barley or rye. With that diagnosis, I was told that I was unable to digest many of the flatbreads and starches that my meals were based around, and that I loved.

What was initially a paralyzing discovery that left me wondering what to eat quietly morphed into an opportunity to eat differently. Spices changed my relationship with food: they promised infinite, tasty combinations where I thought I had none. Suddenly, an egg became a thousand other things, depending on the spice blend used.

It is not easy traveling as a celiac. There are times when it is culturally inappropriate to turn down food because the local population would see it as an insult to their hospitality. I've tried to walk a fine line between eating through a country at a local level and getting myself "glutened" in the process.

While travel for those with dietary restrictions is more complicated than for those with an "everything goes" diet, these limitations can also become opportunities to meet and connect with others. In my case, technology has helped connect me with expats or locals who suffer from the same intolerance.

The Bottom Line: Every Meal Counts

I believe that every meal counts, and that each meal can be seen as a gateway to understanding the environment, economics and politics of the countries you visit. Once you figure out the rules for finding food in a new country, your mealtimes will become a joyful exercise in selective eating, surprising tastes and memories to last a lifetime.

Me and Mrs. Pa next to her smoothie stand in Chiang Mai, Thailand.

Jodi Ettenberg

Paradise in Shoulder Season

After climbing volcanoes in Indonesia I wanted to go somewhere where I could relax by the beach before I moved on. It was late August and having already been in Indonesia for several months, I was looking for a different destination, somewhere beautiful but quiet, and not too full of people. I chose Malaysia's Perhentian Islands because they shut down once the monsoon rains arrive in September, and I thought I might be able to negotiate a lower price since the high season was already over.

After wandering the length of Perhentian Kecil (kecil means "tiny" in Bahasa Indonesia, the local language, so I didn't have far to go), I found a guesthouse at the far end of the beach. Because it was both shoulder season - the weeks between the high tourist season and the rains or cold - and a long term stay, they were willing to provide a sizeable discount on the accommodation. In their words, they lowered the high season prices for the last month before the rains began, keeping the property full but providing travelers with a discount because of the quickly changing weather.

An upside to my time on Kecil? Shoulder season brought beautiful sunsets as the storms rippled past the islands, bathing the beach and the surrounding trees in golden light at dusk. Since my weeks on Kecil, I have made sure to find out when official high season ends and to try to negotiate rates for a shoulder season stay wherever I go. It's proven a reliable money-saver over the years.

Shoulder season on Perhentian Kecil.

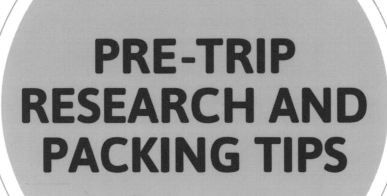

PRE-TRIP RESEARCH AND PACKING TIPS

Tackling the Basics

Before delving into the practical tips for sourcing food safely, it is important to set out some of the basics in planning and preparing for a food-filled journey.

Preparing ahead of time – be it from another country or from home – is important because it offers you some additional peace of mind when you arrive. In the swirling noise and sensory overload of a market in a new destination, I find there is comfort in having done some research.

Yes, it might be chaotic and you might not know where to start once you get off the plane. You might find yourself in a bus parking lot with an alarming number of chickens milling about, or you might get off a train and feel pressure from the mass of people jockeying for you to pick them for local transportation. But if you have done some preliminary reading and preparation, at least you will know that you are not really that lost. You will know the food that people eat; you will have researched how they do so. It is a wonderful place to start.

First Things First: Where Do You Want to Go?

I find the most helpful first step in tackling a journey is to ask yourself a broad set of questions about what you hope to get from your destination. If the answer is "everything!" that is fine too. If you have specific desires, however, it gives you a useful starting point for focusing your research. In narrowing down the particulars of what you find enticing, you will give yourself a bit of structure upon arrival.

Does a food or spice or thread of culture stand out for you? Learning through that item is one way to decide where you want to explore.

For example: ketchup enthusiasts, tracing the roots of this popular condiment, would follow a route from the United States to China and beyond. The original meaning of the word ketchup derived from a Fujian phrase for "fish sauce," used almost 500 years ago. When British and Dutch spice merchants arrived in Southeast Asia in search of spices and other riches, they discovered Fujian ketchup in Indonesia, traded by Chinese merchants.

After bringing the strange sauce back to the UK, attempts were made to reproduce it at home. From a 1742 London cookbook:

> To Make KATCH-UP that will keep good Twenty Years. Take a Gallon of strong stale Beer, one Pound of Anchovies wash'd and clean'd from the Guts, half an Ounce of Mace, half an Ounce of Cloves, a quarter of an Ounce of Pepper, three large Races of Ginger, one Pound of Eschallots, and one Quart of flap Mushrooms well rubb'd and pick'd; boil all these over a slow Fire till it is half wasted, and strain it thro' a Flannel Bag; let it stand till it is quite cold, then bottle and stop it very close.[2]

Charting your trip to follow the historical journey of ketchup is but one example of a food-inspired itinerary.

Do you want to plan around the weather? Traveling during shoulder season can provide the best of both worlds when it comes to food. Often, some of the next season's produce is already on the market. The country guides on the Travel Independent website are a good resource for weather and seasons around the world: travelindependent.info/stories.

Do you want a unifying subject for your food adventures? Are you looking for a soup tour of Asia or a hamburger-a-day in Europe? There are many themed food options to pick from. If you are looking for a series of soup discoveries, Myanmar might be a sound pick. If you are hoping to sample unique pancakes, I would send you to Bali, where they are crepe-thin and made with rice flour, dyed green with pandan leaf and topped with slices of banana. Each country has its own artfully distinct way of creating food, and it can be a fun tactic to plan your itinerary. This theme-based system is ideal for shorter trips as well, focusing on learning about Port in Porto or grilled meat in Argentina or Brazil. Setting a food goal gives you a structure to work with as you plan your days.

Do you want to travel based on what foods are in season? If you already know some of the fruit or foods that appeal, you can plan the timing of your trip around them. I personally love mangosteens, and their season begins in late April in most of Southeast Asia. I planned my departure from Thailand around making sure I would get my fill of my favorite, deep purple fruit.

Mango Season in India

Eating with the seasons brings its share of historical info and learning: mango season in India, for example, when people get worked up into a frenzy over the fruit. An article in the New York Times described the passion India has for its sweet mangoes:

> Mangoes are objects of envy, love and rivalry as well as a new status symbol for India's new rich. Mangoes have even been tools of diplomacy. The allure is foremost about the taste but also about anticipation and uncertainty: Mango season in the region lasts only about 100 days, traditionally from late March through June; is vulnerable to weather; and usually brings some sort of mango crisis, real or imagined.

> ...In Mumbai, many people insist on eating Alphonsos and might even be offended by the suggestion that any alternative could suffice. In New Delhi, on the other hand, many residents belittle the Alphonso and favor the varieties grown in northern India. Almost every state has its own mango jingoism; if love of mangoes is nearly universal in India, so is disagreement over which variety is best.[3]

The zeal for mango season in India is passed down from one generation to the next. I first tried mangoes in elementary school at the home of a classmate whose parents were born in India. They would talk of huge family gatherings to eat the fruit and how eating too many would, their grandmothers warned, cause pimples. They remained nostalgic for the perfect sweetness of the mangoes in India now that they were living in Canada. Exploring a country through its food stories is a rewarding endeavor, and traveling when those foods are in season is a good way to start.

Ripe mangoes, ready for eating.

Food Customs and Quirky Food Etiquette

One of the more fascinating aspects of local food culture is the etiquette and customs behind it, often deeply intertwined with the dominant religion. I have included a list of some of these customs below, as well as some resources at the back of the handbook for learning more in specific destinations.

These are especially fun to use as comparison points when you are traveling with kids. I love watching traveling families explain the reasons why you never plant your chopsticks in a bowl of rice with the points facing down in Japan, or why it is important to eat with your right hand in Malaysia or Indonesia.

Being unaware of the customs is not the end of the world, but by observing and taking note of them, you are equipping yourself with a springboard to more in-depth understanding.

In Italy, cappuccino is meant to be drunk only before a meal, usually before noon. Explanations abound: the milk in the late afternoon can be upsetting to your stomach, it will ruin your appetite before dinner, or it will make you feel bloated after you eat. Regardless of why, Italians tend to imbibe their cappuccinos in the morning, and espressos or other quick shots of coffee later on in the day. According to Rebecca Winke from Brigolante Umbria in Italy: "When you hear the 'only before noon' rule, what that mostly means is that cappuccino is never consumed after a meal – lunch or dinner. You can get an espresso *(caffè)* or, if you really want to live on the edge, an espresso with a dollop of foamed milk *(caffè macchiato)*. Anything milkier than that and you are branding yourself as a clueless foreigner to anyone in a 50-yard radius."

On the Indian subcontinent, Malaysia, Indonesia and several African countries, eating with your left hand is frowned upon. The left hand is generally seen as unclean, as it is used to clean up after bodily functions. Right hands are associated with eating and left hands with bathroom rituals and other cleaning ablutions. Many foods in the region - roti, rice and chicken, vegetable curries and more - are served to be eaten by hand. I am a lefty and I would actually sit on my left hand in order to remember not to eat with it. On a visit to Kuala Lumpur, I was dining with an international businessman, a friend of a friend. Engrossed in conversation, I forgot to sit on my left hand and I started eating with it instead. "What are you doing?" he asked, face aghast. I quickly switched, realizing my mistake, and explained that I was a lefty so technically I might want to avoid my right hand, correct? Laughing, he responded, "Only if you are a dirty girl!" That answered that, and from then on I was more careful.

Thailand's cutlery options include a spoon and fork, chopsticks, or your hands, depending on the meal. Customarily, rice-based dishes in Thailand are eaten with a spoon and a fork, with the spoon as the star of the show. You use your fork to push the food onto the spoon and eat using the spoon only, which is the best way to pick up the most rice in one shot. Depending on the type of food you are consuming, you may also find yourself using chopsticks or your hands. Chopsticks are usually only available when eating noodle soups, or when you are in a Chinese restaurant. For soups, Thais often pick up the noodles with the chopsticks and curl them in a spiral on the spoon, then dip the spoon into the broth before eating. If you see chopsticks at a food stall table, you can safely assume that there will be a noodle soup dish on the menu. In the Northeast of Thailand (also called Isaan), food is frequently eaten with the right hand and sticky rice is used to scoop up the salad or dips. There are many options and much to try.

In Jordan, you will continue to get coffee refills when drinking with Bedouin – until you shake your cup. When guests enter a Bedouin tent, they are invited to coffee. The tradition includes three cups: one for the guest *(Daif)*, one for the soul *(Kaif)*, and one for the sword *(Saif)*. I learned quickly that the cup would be refilled time and time again until I shook it slightly to indicate that I was finished. To do so, you outstretch your arm with cup in your hand (not on your palm) and gently shake it from side to side three times. On my most recent trip to Jordan, my shaking skills obviously needed some work, as I was asked to practice the shaking until my Bedouin hosts were convinced that I got it right.

Cardamom-infused coffee from Jerash, Jordan.

It is customary to gesture to a stranger at the beginning of a meal in Ghana, inviting them to eat with you. When you sit down to eat in Ghana and there are people nearby, it is polite to tell them "you are invited" and gesture down to your food to show them that they are welcome to have some. There is no expectation for you to actually *give* them food, but it is understood that you will offer.

You should not eat off a stacked plate in Thailand. My Thai friends gently informed me that eating off a plate stacked atop another plate is considered bad form. The practice is associated with temple ceremonies for those who have died, and eating off stacked plates is seen as serving the deceased. While I regularly ate at narrow tables in Thailand, I made sure to only stack my plates once the meal was done, to avoid this faux pas.

In Japan and much of Southeast Asia, it is impolite to place your chopsticks vertically in your food or rice, or do the same with a meat or satay skewer. Instead, position your chopsticks or skewer on the side of the plate when not using them. This custom (like the stacking of plates) also stems from funeral rites for the deceased, the vertical placement is how a bowl of rice is offered to spirits at a Buddhist altar, or on a person's deathbed.

Passing food from chopstick to chopstick is also frowned upon in Japan. This is because bones are often passed from chopstick to chopstick after funeral rites in the country.[4]

Showing your teeth when using a toothpick is not polite in many cultures in Southeast Asia. As a friend once said, "You wouldn't floss your teeth in front of the table, so why would you show them your teeth when using a toothpick?"

Food sounds differ depending on the country you are in. In North America and most of Europe it is considered rude to slurp your noodles or make smacking food noises as you eat. Conversely, in parts of Asia it is a sign that you are enjoying the food, and a compliment in its own way. Watch and listen to ascertain what works at the table, then do as the locals do.

In Mongolia, you are expected to drink your tea while holding your cup from the bottom, not from the rim. In addition, when receiving tea or *airag* (fermented mare's milk), you should give and receive your cup with your right hand extended and the left hand supporting the right elbow. Many more quirky and interesting rules exist: you cannot put your tea down on the table until you've had your first sip, you are not supposed to stick your feet out in front of you while you eat, and you should not walk between the two supporting beams in a *ger* (yurt), or pass anything in that space. If you are offered a drink you should accept it, but you do not necessarily need to drink it. Instead, you can dip your right ring finger into the cup and flick your finger above your head, offering a taste to the gods.

In Russia, it is polite to put your wrists on the edge of the table (not in your lap or far into the middle of the table) while eating, and keep your fork in your left hand and knife in your right. And then there is the drinking: "Opposite what many write on the Internet, Russians don't mix vodka with juices or soda. Where some get this idea is unknown, because in Russia it would be considered as an insult to your host to mix your vodka with something else. A toast is pure vodka and it is not sipped. Sipping is also an insult. You down the entire glass; thankfully it's a shot glass, with one swallow."[5]

In Bolivia, office buildings empty out at 10:00 a.m. and 5:00 p.m., for snack breaks. Eating while walking or driving around is frowned upon – both are deemed impolite. Instead, most of the country takes a break mid-morning (for *meriendas*) and late afternoon (for *tecito*) and people head out for fried or baked eats like *salteñas*, which resemble empanadas. Small stands are packed to the gills, and then in a flash they are empty once more.

These are some examples of the many fun quirks that you will discover as you travel, by watching those who eat around you and asking questions about why people do what they do. The list is by no means exhaustive, but I wanted to share some of these traditions because they are part of what makes travel so interesting.

Buddhist offering on a street in Siem Reap, Cambodia.

For more, the resource links at the end of the handbook allow for searching by specific country. Whether you find these customs silly or fascinating or different, abiding by them is a mark of respect and becomes yet another way to connect with locals, who customarily appreciate the effort you are making to fit in. The same tactics work well when the language gap is seemingly insurmountable; observing, respecting and behaving according to custom can be another route to increased understanding.

Dressing the Part as You Travel

I should note that food as an icebreaker or tool to connect with locals cannot be truly successful if you are dressed inappropriately for your location. While in some countries people do not mind if you are dressed liberally, in others the locals will appreciate a more conservative packaging, something more in keeping with the way they dress themselves.

I'm not advocating completely swathing yourself in local attire, but rather that you take a look around and see how locals are dressed. Ignoring the generally-practiced levels of modesty can be perceived as disrespectful. I have found that it is best to err on the side of covering more, rather than less, especially as a solo female traveler. A bonus: for destinations like Myanmar or India, often that clothing becomes a souvenir to take home.

General Etiquette Is Important Too

Dressing the part is one of many ways to fit in. Following general rules of etiquette also goes a long way. Whether it be tipping (is it customary, do people expect it?), handing business cards over with one, two or a specific hand, or a recognition that some of the conventionally accepted gestures from home might mean something different abroad, pre-trip research helps demystify the workings of your destination. The resources section at the back of this handbook includes further readings for these general etiquette rules.

How Do Travelers See a First-Time Visit to North America?

Etiquette rules are not only an interesting way to learn about a new destination but they also provide a fascinating perspective on our own countries, as seen through those who might come and visit from afar.

A perfect example is found in the Wikipedia article on etiquette in North America. According to their "In Restaurants" section, "It is appropriate to contact the waiter by making eye contact, nodding the head, or holding up the index finger. If necessary, "Excuse me..." or, if known, saying the waiter's name is appropriate. Shouting for, snapping fingers at, or whistling for the waiter's attention is rude."[6]

This is in contrast to Myanmar, for example, where kissing at or clapping your hands at the waiter is usually the way people get his or her attention, and is not seen as rude.

My Burmese Longyi: The Perfect Icebreaker

On my second day in Myanmar I decided to find myself a Burmese *longyi*. Little did I know it would turn out to be the best icebreaker I could have asked for. The *longyi* is a sarong-like tube of fabric worn by both genders in different patterns and styles. For women, anything goes in terms of fabrics: beautiful, bright batik patterns, traditional woven zigzags called *acheiq*, stripes or flowers.

Women tie the *longyi* by pulling all of the fabric to one side, folding it back at the hip and tucking it into the opposite side of the waist, usually topped with a fitted blouse worn just to the waistband. They also sew in a thin band of black fabric at the waist. I was told this was "for the sweat," but I found it handy to figure out which side was up.

I decided to get a *longyi* when I realized how prevalent they were. Almost everyone wears the long traditional skirt, and as a solo traveler I thought it would help me blend in. Stepping out of my hostel on that second day, I took out a map to figure out where the market was. Within seconds, shadows cast over the paper and I looked up in surprise to find five women standing there with beaming smiles. "How can I help you?" one of them asked. I explained I wanted to find myself a *longyi*, and the next thing I knew I was holding hands with two of them and on my way to the fabric store.

I wore my *longyi* the next day, and for many days after that. I bought a second one in the traditional Kayin diamond pattern and both proved incredibly useful in Myanmar. On bus rides, drivers would smile and point at the skirt, foisting food upon me at our brief rest stops. In the Kachin state, I attended the annual State Fair with tens of thousands of Kachin from around the world for several days of music, dancing, costumes and rice wine. Wearing my *longyi* one afternoon, I suddenly felt someone undo it from the side. Grasping the fabric and whipping around, I found a group of Kachin women dressed in silver-laden traditional costumes giggling hysterically. Apparently, I had tied it on the wrong side of my torso and – of course – they found my mistake very funny. Cut to a series of group shots, the women doing my makeup in the middle of a dirt road and serving some mohinga (soup) for good measure. It made for an incredible afternoon.

At Inle Lake, I wore the *longyi* yet again when I visited the local markets at dawn. The Pa-O tribeswomen who had descended from the Shan Foothills to buy their food for the week would gawk at it, many coming up to touch the fabric or stare at me unabashedly. A few complimented me on my Burmese style, others would merely point from afar, but it proved to be both an excellent icebreaker and a way to take pictures without seeming too obtrusive.

Overall, trying to blend in was one of the best things I did during my weeks in Myanmar. Of course, I could never look truly Burmese but the surprise and smiles on people's faces made it a wonderful experience. As the captain of one ferry I took down the Irrawaddy said, "With your *longyi*, you are almost a Burmese girl. Welcome!"

Me with Pa-O tribeswomen off of Inle Lake, Myanmar.

Packing Suggestions

There are many resources addressing packing and planning for long-term or short-term travel. I have included checklists at the end of the book, but wanted to highlight some specific items you might want to bring with you and tasks you might want to complete before you go.

Of course, your bag will not be limited to the list below, but this book would be incomplete without some mention of must-haves:

Foldable chopsticks. Some travelers swear by a spork, but I love my portable chopsticks. They unscrew into four pieces, take up no room (and little weight) and are a terrific way to ensure that your utensils are clean. As I note in the safety section below, sometimes the culprit in food-related illness is not the food itself, but rather the way in which the cutlery is washed.

A first-aid kit and a plan for buying medication on the road. My first-aid kit is fairly standard – bandages, gauze, tweezers, antibiotic cream, sutures, burn gel and more but it also has some specific medication for treatment of food-borne illnesses.

I keep it stocked with ciproflaxacin for general bacterial stomach infections, metronidazole for giardia or amoebic dysentery, and loperamide (Imodium) for diarrhea (but only to take if absolutely needed). Each is to be used in consultation with a local doctor, but it is helpful to have them with you in the event that you are isolated and far from medical care. While my initial prescriptions for these medications were filled in North America, I have picked them up for reasonable prices in Mexico, Thailand, and other parts of the world. A chain pharmacy is your best bet for trying to ensure the medication is not counterfeit if you do find yourself looking to fill prescriptions on the road. With respect to malaria, consult your doctor and the malaria maps provided by the Centers for Disease Control and Prevention (cdc.gov/malaria/map) to ascertain whether you should be taking a prophylactic.

Vaccinations. Vaccinations will vary depending on destination. Consultation with a doctor is always a wise idea. For my years of round-the-world travel, I kept the following shots up to date:

- Hepatitis A
- Hepatitis B
- Meningitis
- Yellow Fever
- Tetanus/Diphtheria booster
- Typhoid
- MMR booster (measles, mumps and rubella)
- Polio

Others such as cholera, rabies, and Japanese encephalitis will be subjective based on budget and destination, and your doctor will be able to help determine how necessary they are.

If you are planning for long-term travel and need to update your vaccinations on the road, Red Cross clinics will frequently provide discounted shots in their travel clinics. For example, the Bangkok Red Cross Traveler's Clinic offers many of the shots listed above, at a lower cost than in North America.[7]

Point It: Traveler's Language Kit. Even if you have a smartphone and can download some of the suggested apps for food and translation, the Point It dictionary will come in handy. A thin book with photos divided by topic (food, medical, body parts, etc.), it serves as an instant translation tool in the form of visual cues. Bonus: when I took the Trans-Siberian trains and shared a compartment with a Russian family who spoke no English, the Point It dictionary provided a way to pass time and communicate. I speak no Russian so I would point to an image in the book and say the word in English, they would do the same in Russian, and then we would share our food with each other. Pictures: bringing people together all over the world.

Acidophilus pills. These will help keep your immune system healthy and also aid in replenishing the good bacteria after a course of antibiotics. They now make acidophilus pills that do not require refrigeration, which is ideal for travel. Alternatively, most yoghurts contains acidophilus, albeit in much lower doses.

Thank-you cards. I have found myself in houses for locally cooked meals or invited to join a family for dinner at a restaurant. In many cases, it would have been rude for me to insist on paying my way or to decline the meal. Instead, I have brought a small token to my hosts (usually dessert) and a handwritten thank-you card. By having a stack of simple, embossed cards on hand, you will be prepared when you want to show thoughtful appreciation for a gift of hospitality.

A headlamp. I use my headlamp at home and abroad. The power might go out while you are eating, the streets may not be as well lit as you expected, or you just might want to read about food in bed. The headlamp is a small and useful thing to include in your bag.

A small plastic doorstop. This too takes up little room in my bag but when I am staying alone in a guesthouse, I wedge it from the inside, at the bottom of my door. It gives me the additional peace of mind to know that I'll be awoken if someone does try to get in the room at night. While it is unlikely that you will actually need it, it can be very comforting for the solo traveler heading to bed.

Duct tape. If your bag was, let's just say, shredded when a moving bus dragged it for several kilometers on the overnight trip from Uyuni to La Paz in Bolivia, you would be able to use duct tape to keep it together until you found a new option. Duct tape is also useful for keeping food and bags of snacks bug-free, and for taping up any holes in your room's screen or mosquito netting. It is best carried when rolled in on itself from the outside to save space, leaving the cardboard tube in the center of the tape roll at home.

Safety whistle. It is lightweight, comes in handy in a multitude of situations where you need to get someone's attention, and is something you can clip onto your bag or daypack to have available if needed. Safety whistles are widely available online or at outdoor or hardware stores.

Pre-made allergy cards. If you have food sensitivities, diets or allergies, it is worth investing in these cards in the local language. See the food allergies section for links and options.

Oral rehydration salts. Like the antibiotics noted above, these are not for everyday use but for those occasions where something causes you to fall ill, be it food-based or otherwise. Oral rehydration salts are readily available at pharmacies both at home and abroad. Added to water and stirred before consuming, they replenish the electrolytes and help with dehydration from stomach illness. I've topped up my supply around the world, and have never found a pharmacy that does not stock them.

Portable water purifier (SteriPEN) or water purification tablets. Bottled water is often available but for those concerned about the environmental impact of all that plastic, or for the times you are unable to find bottled water, a SteriPEN or water purification tablets (found at outdoor stores) are ideal for ensuring safe drinking water.

My headlamp and doorstop, always in my bag.

Packing suggestions for foodies with young kids. Christine Gilbert, publisher of almostfearless.com travels with her husband and young son Cole and offers the following advice for kid-friendly packing:

> We travel with two things at all times: snacks and kid-friendly bowls/cutlery. We love to eat locally but that often means spicy food or things that aren't easy for a toddler to bite into. We'll order a local dish with rice, put some of the plain rice aside for our son, and if we're eating street food – like those wonderful kabobs or chicken skewers – we'll cut that up into small pieces to feed to him. It makes a big difference when you are getting a $1 plate of food, to be able to pull aside the child-friendly bits and still enjoy your meal. We also always pack lots of snacks, including fruit. Dehydration can be a problem in warmer climates, and we've found fruit is a way to get him more liquids without chugging water.

Insurance Companies for Travel

I travel with both travel medical and general loss of possession insurance, though some travelers opt to go with one or the other. While those taking shorter trips might have extended coverage from policies at home, it is always prudent to make sure that you are covered in the event of medical emergencies. In addition, if you are sick abroad and treatment is not working, remember that you can always call your insurance company and doctor at home for options. Insurance provides an extra layer of precaution that will go a long way to making you feel more comfortable on the road.

The resources section at the back of this book lists some options and comparison charts for different travel medical insurance plans.

Jodi Ettenberg

ON THE ROAD
WITH AN
APPETITE FOR
NEW FOOD

Food Sourcing and Food Safety: A Strategy for Eating

All of the planning in the world can't prepare you for the wonderful and overwhelming cornucopia of newness you will find when you reach your destination. But whether at markets or supermarkets, ports or bustling squares, you still need to find food when you travel. Moreover, you want it to be food you can trust.

I have provided a two-step strategy below, combining to form an excellent trajectory toward delicious eats that won't break the bank (or your stomach).

First: locate the food. This section of the handbook focuses on the creative ways you can source cheap eats on the road, from recommendations to tips to fun smartphone apps that will make the "finding" part a little easier. It also highlights some of the moral quandaries you might face in trying new foods as some may challenge your personal ethics.

Second: evaluate the safety of the food itself and whether or not the preparation is hygienic. Not all stalls, markets or restaurants are created equally, and a discerning eye goes a long way to keeping your stomach feeling good. This section of the handbook offers up tried and tested suggestions for selecting the cleanest and freshest food sources.

Arepa Arguments in Colombia

I traveled to Colombia as part of a work contract that had me visiting six countries in three weeks, running to meetings like I was participating in the Amazing Race - without the amazing part. My time in Colombia was particularly short: a few nights in Bogota, followed by one night in Medellin. My personal mission was to find the best cheese arepa - a spongy corn flour bread found in parts of South America - in the vicinity. I did not take this task lightly.

I was hopping from meeting to meeting to conduct presentations about an international school in New York, and thus I was dressed in a suit and taking taxis. It was not my usual travel style but I maximized my limited exposure to cabbies by finding out where they liked to eat. I speak Spanish, and aggressively quizzed each driver about where the best arepas were. Each time, the same scene: confusion, suspicion ("Why are you so interested in arepas – you're a tourist in a suit!") and then joy when they realized I really did want to know their answer.

During my few days in Colombia I ate many arepas, but the most memorable was in Bogota. I was dropped off at my guesthouse one day, and as I walked toward the gate, the driver sprang out of the door and shouted after me, "Remember, don't listen to anyone else – the best arepas are not in La Candelaria!"

The guesthouse owner was standing on the porch and heard the driver's bellowing farewell. Within seconds, she had rushed down to the taxi. "What? Why are you telling her lies? I told her to go directly to La Candelaria – after she tries the arepas next door to our hotel, which are the best in the city."

Cue a loud, visceral screaming match, followed by the driver jumping back in the cab and speeding off.

I got my fill of cheese arepas during those few days in Bogota, but I have to say that none were as memorable as the argument that preceded them.

The Circle-Back Routine

How do you make the most of what you eat when you arrive in a new place?

My general rule is to try everything, or at least as much of it as my allergies will allow, in small quantities. I'll try it once even if it looks off-putting; some of the best foods I have sampled have exploded with flavor upon first bite but were not exactly easy on the eyes. The miniature portion size means that if I don't like it, I don't have to eat it. More importantly, it means I won't offend the chef or food cart operator if I leave some behind. If I do like the food – and let's be honest, I normally do – I circle back for another meal later on in my trip.

The initial recommendations I receive are usually suggestions from taxi drivers who want to help me figure out precisely what to eat. As I've illustrated, sometimes their enthusiasm turns into a heated discussion about where to find the best food.

A Note About Condiments

When eating abroad, or eating foreign food at home, it is important not to forget the condiments. Many dishes might seem complete, but condiments and herbs are what round out the tastes for your plate. Among them, don't miss the quintessential Thai tray of hot chili, sour vinegar, salty fish sauce and sweet sugar; the Vietnamese *nuoc cham* dipping sauce and piles of fresh herbs and lettuce; Turkey's wondrous array of pickles; South Korea's pickled vegetables and kimchi; chutneys and pickles in India, Sri Lanka, Pakistan and Nepal; hot salsas in Mexico; *pebre* in Chile; *ají* in Peru, Ecuador or Colombia; or spicy *sambal* in Indonesia and Malaysia.

In fact, a perfect way to introduce yourself to locals is to ask how to eat a dish the way they do.

Moreover, not only should the condiments be tasted, but learning about them and how they came to be used in the local cuisine adds an interesting angle to your food exploration. While the Turkish table includes the same salt and pepper we're accustomed to in North America and Europe, it also houses a tiny jar of chili powder and, inevitably, something pickled. *Turşu*, as they are known, are a fact of life in Turkey and considered a necessity for most meals.

The options aren't limited to cucumber pickles either; very little is off-limits for pickling in Turkey. Cucumbers, eggplant, cabbage, chilies, carrots, onions – you name it, all pickled in grape vinegar, salt and spices. There are even stores where you can bring your produce and pick it up later, pickled to your satisfaction.

Pickling was historically a way to preserve food for long journeys. It deepened the flavor of the vegetable and injected some needed vitamins into your meal: during the fermentation process, bacteria produce vitamins as they digest vegetable matter, which can result in enriched end products.[8] Exploring this smaller side note to Turkish cuisine allows you to learn about the country's attitudes toward food and their taste preferences as a whole.

Tableside pickles from Istanbul, Turkey.

66 Condiments aren't merely finishing touches: they are bridges, borders, redeemers, portals, fingerprints, lifelines. How many times has a mediocre meal on the road-rice and beans in Costa Rica, a Copenhagen hot dog, an anemic stir-fry at a Thai hostel-been saved by a sweet or spicy or savory squirt of something? Bad dishes bathe in the reflected glory of a brilliant condiment.

Shake or squirt, spoon or scatter, condiments do more than boost flavor; they give the diner a hand in the meal. When I've been on the road for a month, away from my kitchen, those jars and bowls and bottles give me a modicum of control in a world otherwise out of my hands. In the most generous countries, in places like Vietnam where great mountains of leaves and citrus and chilies invariably fill your table, you almost feel like you cooked your own meal.

When I travel, I don't buy t-shirts or trinkets; I go to the supermarket and buy the most common condiments I can find, the ones that loom large in local pantries. As a result, my kitchen cabinet is like an edible map of the world: romesco from Catalonia, ponzu from Japan, hulking bottles of amber fish sauce from southern Vietnam. When life keeps me grounded and I start to get anxious, I can be transported, if only for a few bites, with a twist of the wrist. **99**

Matt Goulding
roadsandkingdoms.com

Chili, lime and garlic, the perfect accoutrements to your meal.

A Note About Beverages

This handbook focuses primarily on food, and I decided not to go into detail about what to drink along with your meal. Beverages merit their own tome, as they too are shaped by a country's landscape, climate and history. I do try them all, including a taste of the local moonshine; drinks (both warm and cold) add another layer of exploration on the road. In moderation, of course.

For more background, I suggest the following books:

- *A History of the World in 6 Glasses*, by Tom Standage
- *Drink: A Cultural History of Alcohol*, by Iain Gately
- *Tea: The Drink that Changed the World*, by Laura C. Martin
- *Uncommon Grounds: The History of Coffee and How It Transformed Our World*, by Mark Pendergrast

Tea steeping at a café in Beijing, China.

General Tips for Sourcing Good, Cheap Food

In eating my way around the world, I have amassed a mental Rolodex of tips to find the best food. The following advice reflects those lessons, as well as guidance from other passionate eaters.

Give yourself a pass for your first meal. The first meal in town will almost always be one of the worst. You are tired and hungry, and you are unfamiliar with your surroundings. As obsessive as I am about making every meal count, even I acknowledge that sometimes you just need to eat. For those first meals, go to your guesthouse and ask where the staff would eat lunch. Upon return, you can report back, "I loved the rice dishes but found the place too touristy – do you have another suggestion?" Inevitably, the guesthouse staff will be excited to see you excited about food, and will help hone your selections during your time there.

Use all the information you have in front of you. When and where does the local population eat? The crowd will follow the freshest foods, and paying attention to what locals do is a boon both for safety and for sourcing what is worth eating. Do they favor a big midday meal with smaller meals at night, as in Myanmar or Jordan? Do they eat a much later evening meal, as in Spain or Argentina? When in Rome...

Don't forget about breakfast. Many travelers stick to breakfasts that resonate with their cultural upbringing, but it is actually a perfect meal in which to go outside your comfort zone. From soups to plates of cucumbers, tomatoes and cheese to porridges and curries, breakfasts abroad vary wildly. Early meals are also reliable times to meet locals in Southeast Asia - many start their day at the markets and eat while they are shopping for fresh produce. In addition, on the Indian subcontinent many inventive eats are only available on the streets at breakfast time. Skipping street food for that meal would mean missing out on many wonderful taste combinations.[9]

Don't ignore local desserts. I would encourage you to embrace whatever creativity is present in the form of dessert, from knafe in Jordan (baked phyllo pastry with sweet cheese and honey) to glutinous rice balls stuffed with red bean paste in China to flavorful taro, coconut and sugar-coated five-cent treats in Thailand. It may not be your traditional apple pie or chocolate, but it is a fun end to a new meal.

Chicken pudding dessert from Istanbul, Turkey. Rich, sweet and tasting of cinnamon and vanilla.

❝ *Lau leans over by the fishmonger's stall, as feisty gray groupers and pink snappers leap and flop manically in their plastic tubs, trying to escape their fate. Cantonese cooking emphasizes seasonal ingredients and natural flavors, so Hong Kongers like to buy their fish, fowl, and meat as fresh as possible. "Fresh" in Hong Kong means that you get to witness the final blow.* **❞**

Daisann McLane
"Ghosts of Hong Kong", National Geographic,
March 2011

Eat what is fresh. If you are staying near the coast, take advantage of your proximity to fish and seafood. You can head down to the harbor and take a look at whether there are restaurants attached to the piers. If not, a seafood market is a second option. In Manila, the owner of my guesthouse took us to a fresh fish and seafood market where we picked out the food we wanted, and then walked upstairs to wait until it was cooked. Eating as close to the harbor as possible is recommended, especially when the country's power grids or refrigeration systems might not function consistently. Remember that when opting for raw foods such as sushi or ceviche, you need to exercise more care as the risk of food-borne illness is heightened. Be sure that the fish is fresh and has been refrigerated since it was caught.

Ask around for the regional dishes that make locals proud. Make use of your pre-trip research and go looking for those not-to-be-missed dishes. Doing so will, as a matter of course, bring smiles and lively suggestions, as Cameron Stauch notes below.

Go to early morning markets. They are good places to see what is happening at ground level with respect to food. Most produce markets in South America and Southeast Asia have restaurant stalls attached, perfect for sampling the local food. In Myanmar, markets rotate throughout Inle Lake, allowing the Pa-O tribespeople to descend from the Shan Foothills and shop for the next five days. Visiting these markets at dawn provided insight into how people ate and shopped for their food, and a place to try the soups and snacks that the Pa-O were buying to fuel their return up the hill after the markets shut down. In Santiago, Chile, La Vega Centrale market offers up mounds of produce, lots of movement and noise and some terrific food.

Return to learn. Even if you go in the morning, don't forget to go back again later during your stay, to see the contrast between the market setting up and how it slows down. You can take stock of the industrious food vendors at work, understand how the farmers get their foods there, and see what the local eateries stock up on for their day, informing your choices for later. These movements and patterns will help you understand how a place treats its food and its mealtimes. If you enjoy photography, the variation in light on the same places at different times of day makes for striking photos.

❝ *Of course, the location of street food shifts over the course of the day too. Our tour took place in a business district between 11:00 a.m. and 2:00 p.m., meaning that the streets were filled with local workers looking for something filling for a late almuerzo or early comida. In the early mornings, women selling atole frequently circulate around transport hubs to provide commuters with a light desayuno. Meanwhile, in the evenings, elote sellers cluster near movie theaters, and other food stands may be set up in parks to cater to a different public than the one served during the day.* **❞**

Nicola Twilley on eating street food in Mexico City
EdibleGeography.com/eating-the-street

Participate in the market shuffle. For Southeast Asia and South America, different foods and produce are sold and eaten at different times of the day. A morning market might close up at noon and reopen at midnight selling freshly cut flowers; an animal auction on Tuesday might be a vegetable market on Thursday. Asking around about when markets open and close and which days particular wares are sold will help familiarize you with what is important on a local level and allow you to plan your days around the offerings.

Smaller towns are a good source of direct access to food. They also provide an opportunity to learn where products come from and where they go. They are much closer to the source, and locals are especially curious about why you would want to eat what they do. For those interested in history and food, these smaller destinations are also the place to ask questions and watch the food being farmed or sold, which provides invaluable insights into a country's food system.

Taxi drivers are an under-utilized source of dining recommendations. If you are looking for food suggestions, the older the taxi driver you approach, the better. Where he eats lunch is often where I want to eat lunch; I have yet to be disappointed by the suggestions I've received. I am careful to ask where the driver ate, not where they think I ought to eat (in doing so, I'm trying to avoid a commission-based recommendation).[10] In terms of breaking the ice, I carry cough drops with me and offer one to my taxi driver immediately upon entering the cab. It is disarming and usually a surprise, and they are much more willing to offer suggestions when they've got candy. Cough drops are the perfect icebreaker, as I note below.

Seek out community bakeries in small Middle Eastern or North African towns. When I was wandering around the old medina in Chefchaouen, Morocco, I saw young men bringing piles of branches to one house in the center. Uncooked, kneaded dough would follow, brought by a young woman. She would hand the bread in through the window, and it would be fed into the big wood-burning oven. Rotating lines of branches, uncooked bread, and cooked bread would follow throughout the day. I realized that there was only one communal bakery for many of the people living in the medina, and families would each knead the dough at home and then bring it to be baked. This bakery is called a *furn* and provides a fascinating layer of shared living to observe as you travel."

One of Chefchaouen, Morocco's many medina alleyways, taken during the Muslim holiday of Eid al-Adha, the Feast of Sacrifice.

Eat at shopping malls, supermarkets or hawker stand food courts in Asia. I love exploring supermarkets when I am somewhere new, and seeing how the food is stocked and the aisles planned. In addition, these stores often sell cheaper versions of local eats, made fresh daily. Food courts atop shopping malls throughout Asia and South America are also full of quick, cheap food, often the same fare you would find outside. In Sydney's Chinatown, you can walk upstairs at a mall and find heaping bowls of *laksa* (coconut spicy soup) and noodles from a wide cross-section of Asian countries. In Singapore, Malaysia and Hong Kong, hawker stalls are fail-safe places for delightful, inexpensive meals.

Save your dinner appetite for nighttime walking streets or markets. Avoid the night markets geared toward tourists (e.g. Dong Hua Men Night Market in Beijing), and instead take a peek at the ones for locals. Often this includes not just markets, but regular streets that become pedestrian walkways in the evening, filled with food. Vientiene's night market in Laos is where many locals go to pick up dinner but it was listed as a 'miss' in my guidebook. It might not have been an exciting sight to see, but it definitely provided me with cheap and fresh dishes to try.

Find a midday meal at a hospital or university. I learned this rule during my travels through South America in 2002: wherever there are universities, there are cheap eats. It is perhaps a universal truth that students are a hungry bunch with small budgets. As a result, the food is usually very reasonably priced. Will it be the best quality meal on your trip? No. But it has been a fail-safe method of sourcing cheaper meals on-the-go without sacrificing taste. Because of the volume of students, the turnover is fast and the food has usually been quite safe to eat. The same sourcing rule applies for hospitals, with plenty of cheap stalls crowded within a few blocks of the hospital building. Note: Finding food adjacent to universities is a valuable option for lunch but ill-advised for dinner when freshly-made food will have been sitting out since the midday meal.

Cooking classes or street food walking tours provide an excellent starting point. For those looking to make a meal and not just eat one, attending a cooking class allows you to try the food and see how it is made, giving you an appreciation of the local cooking. It also gives you access to a knowledgeable foodie in the form of your instructor, who can guide you toward local eats in town.[12]

Finding Food Through Locals in India

Chef and culinary interpreter Cameron Stauch has spent many months eating his way through India. In this story, he explains how his curiosity for trying local foods led to a series of suggestions about where to find them.

Upon my first taste I immediately fell for India and its amazing cuisines. But with so many people and so many restaurants -- from *dhabas* to *darshinis* to streetside *chaatwallahs* -- finding safe and delicious food was at times a challenge for me. My time spent traveling around the different regions of India made one lesson clear: figuring out whose advice to follow about where to eat was just as important as deciding what I would eat once I got there.

Fortunately, as I traveled India, I routinely encountered locals who were forthright with their suggestions about where to eat, what regional specialties to try and, most importantly, what to avoid. More often than not, a local resident will suggest to you spots that are well established and have a loyal following.

I fondly recall an early June visit to Bangalore, where following some local culinary advice reaped delicious rewards. As usual, I reached the main market at dawn, with women in silk saris wearing turmeric colored Sampige flowers woven in their hair selecting fragrant garlands for their daily prayers along with fresh produce for their evening meal. *Dhoti*-clad Brahmin men were visiting one of the many Hindu temples which dot the neighborhood. It was here in Malleswaram, in the middle of chaotic Bangalore, that I discovered a vegetarian culinary oasis.

My friend Ragu recommended that for lunch I visit Halli Mane, which in the local Kannada language means "village home." Located on a side street, and built to resemble a rural village house with pillars and terracotta tiles for the roofing, I had to elbow my way through the hungry crowds to place my order. Halli Mane is unique in that its menu regularly features traditional dishes of rural Karnataka. Some of these signature dishes are made with a locally grown grain called ragi, or finger millet. Ragi is a hardy grain, easy to grow, cheaper to buy, and more nutritionally balanced than rice. Consequently, dishes such as *ragi roti* and *ragi mudde* are important elements in the diets of farmers and villagers on the interior plains of Karnataka. I was eager to try *ragi mudde*, best described as a tennis ball-sized steamed dumpling. Mischievous grins were directed my way as the other diners watched me curiously as I tried this unusual dish. Thankfully, one young woman explained how I should pinch off a small marble-sized piece from the dough ball and dunk it in a spicy soup made of tamarind and greens. I quickly learned that she had forgotten to share one essential step: swallow the piece whole because chewing the dough makes it stick to your teeth.

Later that day, wandering along bustling Margosa Road, I saw a long line of people waiting patiently outside a small *darshini*, a vegetarian fast food outlet, and Bangalore's response to the introduction of Western fast food in the 1980s. Another dozen or so people were off to the side eating in a state of silent delight. Peeking through the opening to see what was for sale, I was greeted by an elderly gentleman with thick glasses balanced on the edge of his nose. I paid him a ridiculously small amount of money and he handed me two plates: one containing piping hot, melt in your mouth *vadas* (fried savory snacks) and the other containing the lightest, most delicate *idlis* (steamed South Indian snacks made from lentils and rice) imaginable – the best I have ever had. And judging from the lines of customers his success, no doubt, allowed him to finance at least part of his son's education.

The following few days in Bangalore I consistently returned to savor the old world charm at those street stalls. With each successive visit I met warm people who, once aware of my openness to try new foods, directed me to some of my most memorable meals.

A Geographical Starting Point for Cheap Eats

Much of this book discusses tips for sourcing cheap, delectable food and ways to choose your meals with safety in mind. But how do you decide which areas of the city to hunt in? Many have their own trail of cultural clues, often in the form of markets and street food haunts. These are good targets to focus on before you hone in using the judicious tips below.

- In **North America** this translates into avoiding restaurant chains and seeking ethnic eats, usually as far away from the financial center or business district as you can manage. Lower rents often translate into lower food prices. As Tyler Cowen notes in An Economist Gets Lunch, "A lot of low-rent places are ugly, but still they might have good food and they are especially likely to have cheap food that isn't junk food."[3] In New York, the outer boroughs provide swaths of adventurous eating areas, from Flushing, Queens' sprawling Chinatown to Mexican eateries off of Main Street, Queens, to the flea markets of Brooklyn. Another interesting option is Conflict Kitchen (conflictkitchen.org), which is a pop-up restaurant serving foods only from those countries that the United States is in conflict with. In addition, Toronto, Austin and Portland are leading a North American food truck movement, and in many places food cart festivals provide endless joy in the form of cheap food. You can even find a variety of smartphone apps to help you search out street food trucks or carts in North American cities.

- In **Europe**, the emphasis should be on smaller markets. Many cities and provinces are turning toward local, organic foods and farmer's markets, and agritourism is on the rise. In Paris alone, there is at least one market (and often several) in each of the twenty arrondisements. Covered markets or restaurant areas like Borough Market in London, Barcelona's La Boqueria and Convention Market in Paris all offer fresh, reasonably priced produce and food in what are large and often expensive cities.

- In **Bangkok**, Soi 38 night market is an excellent street food choice, Chinatown's seafood restaurants allow you to choose your food before it is cooked, and there are often clusters of food stalls with fast turnover near most BTS (SkyTrain) stations.[4]

- Hawker stalls in **Singapore** are plentiful and a clean, safe way to indulge in street food. Gourmet eStorie (gourmetestorie.com) has reviews and recipes to help you parse the options.

- In **Hanoi**, resident Mark Lowerson recommends a little narrow alley called Ngõ Đong Xuân, running from Hàng Chieu to Cau Đông in Hanoi's Old Quarter.[15]

- In many **Southeast Asian capitals** there is often a "Little India" district, and the food is wonderful in Malaysia, especially in Kuala Lumpur and Penang.

- **Mong Kok** in the Yau Tsim Mong District of Hong Kong's Kowloon has more than its fair share of cheap eats.[16]

- **Djemaa el Fna** in Marrakesh's old medina boasts stalls of grilled merguez, fresh seafood and meats and harira soups.

- On any given day in **La Vega Centrale in Chile** you will see street stalls piled high with pumpkin bread called *sopaipillas*, as well as your choice of the Completo, a hot dog topped with a shocking amount of mashed avocado, mayonnaise and tomato.

Lunchtime tacos from a market in Mexico City's central business district.

Walking Tours to Guide Your Food Choices

The walking tour is another interactive food-based option for exploring cities around the world. They provide a good, comfortable overview of a destination's food culture, and a helpful framework for conducting your own post-tour discovery. Some ideas are listed below, but guidebooks customarily suggest street food tours if they are available. Another suggestion is to check Chowhound.com, where food enthusiasts often share "trip reports" from their travels.

- Penang: Helen Ong's food tours, helenong.com
- Ho Chi Mihn: Back of the Bike Tours, backofthebiketours.com
- Beijing: market tours, tea tastings and cooking courses with The Hutong, thehutong.com
- Chiang Mai: Farm School cooking classes, thaifarmcooking.net
- Bangkok: Bangkok Food Tours, bangkokfoodtours.com
- Mexico City: Eat Mexico food tours, eatmexico.com
- Hanoi: Sticky Rice Street Tours, stickyrice.typepad.com/ street_food_tours
- Istanbul: Istanbul Eats Walks istanbuleats.com/walks-2
- Shanghai: Culinary Backstreets' walking tours culinarybackstreets.com/culinary-walks

Marrakesh's busy market square, Djemaa el Fna, at night.

Using Technology to Make Finding Food Easier

Blogger Phil Paoletta notes below that he often turns to Twitter and Facebook for food suggestions. For those using technology when traveling, these social networks - as well as websites like eGullet and Chowhound - provide some tried and tested feedback for what to do where, and what to eat. I have solicited restaurant suggestions in Chicago, Sydney and Bangkok on Facebook and tweeted questions about a particular dish in Morocco, and received helpful responses each time.

Another option is to attend pre existing meet ups. Couchsurfing.org and Meetup.com both offer ways of connecting with like-minded groups around the world. While I'm a member of Couchsurfing, I have not used the service to stay at anyone's house. Instead, I've benefited from their chapter happy hours or get-togethers, where expats (hosts) and travelers mingle and swap stories. The meetups have been a good source of food finds, as they allow for direct access to people living in the city. Meetup.com is another means of finding friendly people looking to eat. The site is also a way to connect with travelers who have niche interests or requirements, e.g. a celiac dining group or a vegetarian group.

For more specific uses:

Apps and Sites to Source Food
- Urbanspoon (free app and site)
- Yelp (free app and site)
- Chowhound.com – reviews from around the world, passionate community of foodies.
- EGullet, forums.egullet.org – a service from the Society for Culinary Arts & Letters, the forums are divided by region and area of interest.
- Local Eats ($0.99, allows you to filter by neighborhood or type of food and includes many international cities).
- Many cities have their own street food-specific guides, available with a quick search in iTunes or Android's app directories. I've used these for New York, Penang and many others.

- Another good source of apps is Sutro Media, with many cities covered: sutromedia.com/apps.html.

Food-Based Social Media

- Foodspotting - share and find food.
- Foursquare - location-based check-ins which recommend nearby places based on geolocation.
- FoBoh - restaurant network, primarily for vendors but interesting to get a feel from the insider's perspective.

Each provides resources for sourcing food with a more personal feel than guidebooks.

Apps to Simplify Your Travels

Finding cheap and tasty food may be the primary goal of this book but there are ways to make communicating what you want easier.

- Translation apps such as ICOON (free), Word Lens ($9.99), Google Translate (free), Hello Hello (free), World Customs (free), and HowCast (video tutorials; free) are a good start, using photos or local language to get across your preferences.
- Currency converters like Oanda (free), or XE (free) allow you to figure out what you are paying in your local currency, and not get the short end of the stick when converting money abroad.
- When you eat too much, the Clothing Size Converter (free) will come in handy to help you find new clothes.
- Tipping guides come in handy too. For Android users, Tipping Bird (free) provides a worldwide tipping guide for over a dozen countries. For iPhone users, GlobeTipping ($0.99) will suggest tipping guidelines for over 200 countries worldwide.
- And finally, the Sit or Squat app (free) for iPhone, with 100,000 listed toilets worldwide will come in handy when you just have to use a washroom and don't know where to find one. For Android users, you can download Bathroom Scout Pro ($1.36), which lists over 600,000 toilets worldwide.

Food Dictionary Apps

- Olis Olois apps offer dictionaries for Japanese, Mexican, Spanish, Thai, Vietnamese and French food, and sushi. ($0.99 each).
- Foodict Food Dictionary ($1.99) has a comprehensive database of international food expressions and definitions.
- Eat the World ($1.99) is a newer app currently building out their picture dictionary of dishes by country, including how they are written in local script.

Navigation Apps

- Google Maps (free)
- EveryTrail (free, GPS app)
- AllSubway ($0.99)
- World Subway Maps ($1.99)
- Around Me (free)

Breaking the Ice with Locals

An important corollary of learning through food is learning from the people who make and eat it, the locals you encounter as you travel.

I've noted throughout this book that interaction with locals often kicks off with a smile or a question, leading to a discussion that is then followed by an invitation. In my experience, these are the impromptu invites to weddings, at-home dinners or community barbecues that I would never have received without making that first move and engaging.

Some small tips to break the ice:

- If you are taking a long bus or boat ride in a developing country, bring a bag of oranges. If oranges are not in season, opt for another small fruit to dole out, kids first. Not sweets. Fruit. (It is always wise to make eye contact with parents to make sure that it's acceptable to hand it over, but as you are giving out fruit, there ought to be little resistance.) At the beginning, there is usually some confusion and reticence but once people realize that you are merely trying to share, they will do the same. By the end of the ride, you will have been generously fed by everyone on board. Some of my more memorable stories and lessons have come from conversations that started with a citrus fruit.

- Carry cough drops for cab drivers, as noted above. They work wonders in winning them over.
- Do you have kids? They might be the best icebreakers. It is always wonderful to watch the interaction between local children and those traveling through, starting with a mutual curiosity and often progressing quickly to a game.

Oranges: your go-to snack for getting from A to B.

- If all else fails? That smile I mentioned earlier. It almost always works. Paul Theroux notes that "in the worst slum in India, the meanest street in Thailand or Cambodia, chances are that a smile will make you welcome."[7]

Travel with Kids

Christine Gilbert, publisher of AlmostFearless.com, on travel with her son Cole:

Our son has completely changed the way we travel. Without exception, he's been our gateway to local life: letting us spend an afternoon in a Muslim home where they only spoke Arabic, but our children played together; teaching me Spanish slang when the waitress held him through our entire meal, sitting next to us and chatting in Spanish; and even opening communication with our shy Thai neighbors who probably would never have spoken with us except for our child. As a mother, it's helped me examine my nervousness at letting strangers hold my baby (you get used to it quickly!) and it just shows you a side of humanity that you wouldn't see otherwise. I remember in Egypt last year, just after the revolution, there were still some angry protests and we were a little nervous -- until we walked around the city and the men, not the women, would run over and grab our child and spin him around and kiss him. I'll never get over the affection for children in some countries.

The Ethics of Eating Certain Foods

Travel does come with its share of ethical considerations. With respect to food, my concerns stems from the types of foods I am eating, and where my money is going when I support a local restaurant. I try to frequent small, family-owned vendors in lieu of larger places.

There are certain food choices that have drawn the ire of critics and conservationists alike. When traveling, it is particularly difficult to ascertain how animals are cared for or where they are sourced. Informing yourself about a country's treatment of animals is important, and so is setting boundaries. Ask yourself: how comfortable are you with eating exotic animals, or animals that are kept as pets at home? Are there limits to what you will and won't try, even if it is local fare?

As an example, eating dog is popular with locals in parts of Vietnam and other parts of Asia. While some people may not have a moral objection to eating one animal (dog) over another (cow or lamb), they may take issue with the way the animals are treated and raised. Thus, deciding not to eat dog in those regions may stem less from an aversion to consuming the animal itself and more from the ethics of its treatment. There are many nuances to these eating decisions. My choices often hinge on the way the animal is treated, but others feel differently. My best advice is to conduct your research and then align the results with your own moral compass.

The United Nations Environmental Programme releases a list of endangered animals yearly, which provides a starting point to answer the questions above.[18] Expats can also guide you with respect to what food consumption is normal and what is for show or for tourists. They can speak to the treatment of animals too, stories that might not make it into the press in North America or Europe.

Case Study: Shark Fin Soup

Background: Shark species have suffered extreme population decline during the last two decades. A main culprit for these deaths is the use of shark in soup, mainly served at banquets and weddings in certain Asian communities within and outside China. An astounding 10.3 million kilograms (22,707,613 pounds) of shark fins and related products were imported into Hong Kong alone in 2011, according to statistics from The Pew Charitable Trusts Environmental Group report "Navigating Global Shark Conservation: Current Measures and Gaps".[19]

In the news: In the last few years, bans on the importation and sale of shark fin products have been on the rise. The bans are gaining speed in part because of shark finning's effect on dwindling shark populations: the fins are cut from sharks, which are often flung back into the ocean. Unable to swim, they die slowly. Several US States have passed legislation against the distribution or importation of shark fins and Venezuela became the first South American country to ban finning in its waters. In early July 2012, China also announced that it would stop serving shark fin at official government banquets, starting in 2015.

Ultimate conclusion: Based on the research, I made the decision to avoid shark fin soup even though it was an authentic dish in several of the countries I visited. While I do love to enjoy food as locals do, this soup crossed a line for me. As I noted above, ultimately it is important to avail yourself of information before you dig in. Just because local cultures eat a dish doesn't always mean you ought to do the same.

Allergies and Special Dining Considerations

The fact that I have celiac disease surprises people who know that I've been writing about food. They assume that if I write about it, I must be able to eat most of it. By necessity, allergies may change the way you eat, but they don't need to keep you at home. There are many tools available to translate the needs you might have, and though some countries are more receptive than others, your food requirements can also forge connections with people you meet as you eat and roam.

Having celiac disease has required me to break down the dishes I'm eating into their component parts and in the process I have learned about how people in countries around the world think about food. In Italy, for example, celiac disease is surprisingly well-received. Like many fellow travelers, I assumed that a country so focused on wheat products would be appalled at a diet without gluten. In fact, when I was first diagnosed with celiac disease, my Italian friend's father proclaimed that a life without pasta was "a fate worse than death." Instead, on my visit I found that Italians are so focused on enjoying the dining experience that a whole subset of allergy-friendly eating has cropped up. From tiny Umbrian towns to bigger cities like Rome, everyone knew what the disease was and exactly what to serve in order to help me avoid getting sick.

Two broad suggestions for less familiar places:

Printable allergy cards.
These are available in a multitude of languages, and for many different allergy or food restrictive situations. I've included some options below, but the list is by no means exhaustive.

- Select Wisely: selectwisely.com/selectwisely/content_pages/order_cards. htm - $8.50, includes "strongly worded card" option
- Allergy Translation: allergytranslation.com/Home/home.php - $8.00 USD, 175 allergies and 11 special diets
- Dietary Card: dietarycard.com – $9.40 USD, 17 languages

• Aller Global: allerglobal.com/index.php?sl=en – free, allows you to create at-home printable allergy cards.

Take advantage of forums before you go.
Celiac.com and other allergy-specific forums include advice from those who have traveled and suggest places to eat. I've included some resources in each section below, but on a more informal basis, questions can be submitted to allergy forums and answered by travelers who have been there before. Meet up groups are concentrated in North America (allergies.meetup.com) but are another useful resource for finding tips for safe travel.

Celiac Disease
While celiac disease is well-known in many parts of North America, Australia and Europe, it is not so everywhere. In addition to the cards above, the following sites have proven extremely helpful in figuring out where to eat on the road.

• Globally Gluten Free's Resources page: globally-glutenfree.com/online-resources
• The Celiac Scene (North America only) dining guide and maps: theceliacscene.com
• Celiac cards from Celiac Travel: celiactravel.com/cards
• List of international celiac societies, always a good resource: celiacdisease.about.com/od/theceliactraveler/a/IntlSocieties.htm
• Celiac.com's list of articles about gluten-free travel: celiac.com/categories/Gluten%252dFree-Travel

Nut Allergies
Nut allergies are no laughing matter, and can affect people to varying degrees. For those with allergies that are life-threatening from a small cross-contamination of peanuts or nuts, research should be undertaken with serious diligence and care to avoid countries where peanuts or nuts are a fundamental part of the cuisine should be considered.

Travis Ball has a severe nut allergy and travels with an epinephrine auto-injector (EpiPen). He is not as sensitive as some but does get extremely ill if he ingests nuts. Here is what he has to suggest:

❝ *Traveling with food allergies can be rough, but you don't need to let that stop you from traveling to countries where you think it might be an issue. If I had let my allergy to peanuts (and all nuts for that matter) stop me from visiting Thailand (a country known for peanut sauces and using nuts in many national dishes), I would have missed out on some great experiences. Conduct your research carefully and be extremely watchful about what you consume – always ask about ingredients before you eat.*

I tend to double check with Wikipedia and foodie friends on what types of food I should be wary of. As for being careful, everyone treats their own allergy differently and tends to be as careful as they need to be. While mine can be life-threatening, I do what I need to do in terms of research and learning to feel comfortable that I'm on top of whatever situation I'm in. The travel cards are a huge asset in places where language can be an issue, but primarily I rely on myself and my own experience and interaction with locals to get me through most situations. It's also good to alert people you are traveling with to your allergy so that others are aware of the issue, just in case. ❞

Travis Ball
flashpackerhq.com

- Tips for travel with a nut allergy: matadornetwork.com/abroad/7-ways-to-cope-with-a-nut-allergy-abroad
- Airline policies with respect to food allergies: foodallergies.about.com/od/outandabout/a/Airline-Food-Allergy-Policies.htm

Vegetarian Travel

Vegetarian travel is harder in some countries than in others, but carrying food cards and learning to say "only vegetables" in the local language will get you a long way. I was vegetarian in the past (for several years) but the celiac disease diagnosis led me to re-introduce meat into my diet. Having traveled with vegetarian friends, I can attest to the willingness of people around the world to help you find the food you need when you ask politely and respectfully. And as Akila from The Road Forks notes below, being vegetarian can itself provide a bonding experience.

For finding vegetarian restaurants abroad:
- Happy Cow: happycow.net
- Vegetarian Phrases from Around the World: ivu.org/phrases
- Country-specific vegan travel guides: circleourearth.com/vegan-travel/vegan-country-guides
- Vegetarian Thai Food Guide: eatingthaifood.com/vegetarian-thai-food
- Vegetarian Restaurant Database: vegetarian-restaurants.net/International.htm
- Vegan Backpacker's Worldwide Guide: veganbackpacker.com/travel-guide
- The Veggie Bus: theveggiebus.org
- Vegetarian Travel: vegtravel.com
- Vegetarian Guides from A Little Adrift alittleadrift.com/category/vegetarian-travel-guides
- Vegetarian Guides from Never Ending Voyage: neverendingvoyage.com/tag/vegetarian

Vegetarian Penang curry, creamy and delicious.

Sautéed broccoli, mushrooms and spices.

Bonding over Vegetarian Food in Zambia

In Livingstone, Zambia, we took a cooking class with Anna, a skinny African woman with beautiful wide eyes and short cropped hair in a polo shirt clearly two sizes too large for her.

We rode to the market together. Squawking chickens and women wearing bright woven chitenges occupied the sprawling stalls and stands well past the tourist area. Most of the vegetables I knew, but some I did not. Anna picked out bunches of *chibwaba* (pumpkin leaves), bitter leaves, and a green leafy vegetable she called rape (which is what we use to make rapeseed oil), dried okra leaves, and sweet potato leaves. We bought some of the vegetables themselves - okra, tomatoes, and onions - but others like sweet potato and pumpkin were considered too rich for daily consumption.

The chicken purchased for my non-vegetarian husband was almost an afterthought. The Zambians do not eat meat on a daily basis and the chicken we purchased - live and very much wishing to escape Anna's steel grip - cost as much as all of the other vegetables and grains together.

We chopped the purchased vegetables under the shade of an acacia tree. Anna laughed when I could not master the Zambian way of cutting greens: a method involving gathering a bunch of the roots in one hand and sharply running the knife blade directly through the vegetable while still held in the air. "Only children use cutting boards," she said, though she gave me a plate to use if I needed it. We cooked the greens using two different preparations: with peanuts and peanut oil, and with tomatoes and onions.

Afterwards, we made *nsima*, the staple of the Zambian diet. *Nsima*, like polenta, pap, and grits, is nothing more than cornmeal poured into boiling water until it forms a thick consistency. The cook uses a wooden paddle rather than a spoon to stir the *nsima* together, resulting in thick, almost doughy wedges. No Zambian woman will marry her son off unless her future daughter-in-law can make a proper batch of *nsima*.

The finished meal was art - the best meal we ate in our three months in southern Africa. Though my husband had chicken at our Zambian feast, meat was not the star. (In fact, my husband later stated that he thought the chicken was too tough, probably because it was not fattened, as chickens are in the United States.) Instead, the vegetarian fare - twenty little bowls of sautéed and steamed greens and vegetables served alongside the creamy *nsima* - tempted and dazzled our taste buds.

Though I will never be able to eat Argentina's famous steaks or Japan's delectable sushi, in Zambia, I ate like a Zambian.

Akila McConnell
theroadforks.com

Fatoush, a colorful salad topped with sumac, lime juice, fresh herbs, pomegranate molasses and olive oil popular in Lebanon, Jordan and other countries of the Middle East.

Other Allergies or Restrictions

The above sections are merely three examples of restricted eating when traveling. There are other allergies and dietary restrictions that exist, whether based on religious beliefs or other factors. Thankfully, there are now online resources that provide information, advice, suggestions and opportunities for interaction and discussion.

How to Eat Cheap Food Safely

The sickest I've been during the past five years, with the exception of the mishap with that llama empanada I mentioned earlier, was in North America, not abroad. Eating safely is absolutely possible, and enjoyable, if you set basic rules.

"But wait!" you might say, "The US Centers for Disease Control and Prevention advises me to avoid eating street food!"

The exact quote is "Avoid eating foods or drinking beverages purchased from street vendors or other establishments where unhygienic conditions are present."[20] The advice assumes that street food is necessarily unhygienic, which is not the case. They are, to be sure, much less standardized in their cleanliness compared to restaurants in the West. But there is also a risk that eating at home might be unsafe.[21]

No one can absolutely guarantee that you will never become ill while traveling. Food-related travel sickness can spring from a variety of factors: rotted meat, unhygienic preparation, improper temperature control, and, of course, lack of attention to appropriate hand-washing.

As a result, the following tips aim to take all of these aspects into consideration; it is wise to follow the crowds and eat with the seasons, but also to take note of the conditions of the stalls you visit, and how the foods are kept.

The last time I got food poisoning was in Thailand, from a small container of yoghurt that was well before its expiration date, and was completely sealed. I spent the night on the floor of the bathroom in my Chiang Mai apartment, half being sick and half laughing at myself. For all the meticulousness I exercised in choosing my meals, I never thought I would be brought down by refrigerated yoghurt.

Whether the store hadn't kept it cold or the yoghurt had been left outside during transportation will never be known, but the first thing I did when I recovered was eat a big bowl of noodle soup, from a street stand in Luang Prabang.

66 *Don't assume that if food is prepared in a restaurant or hotel kitchen it's "safer" than food prepared on the street. My last major bout of street food-itis, three years ago, was actually the result of dinner at a fancy Singapore hotel.*

Street food's major advantage is transparency: where else but the street can you check out the cook's hygiene and the cleanliness of prep surfaces, see how ingredients are stored, and observe how your food is cooked? Rarely in a restaurant, never in a hotel. When it comes to eating safely your eyes are your friend and the best place to put them to use is on the street. **99**

Robyn Eckhardt
Food and travel journalist, eatingasia.typepad.com

The biggest rule of all: go with the flow of people. Is a street stall packed? Chances are, with such a high turnover the food will be far fresher than elsewhere. You don't want to be eating food that has been sitting around for hours, especially at a restaurant buffet, as it will have a higher chance of being invaded by bacteria.

Take a closer look at the stall you want to patronize. In sourcing street food, taking a close look at the vendors themselves is an important step. Try to avoid vendors who chop food and also handle money unless there is a hands-free mechanism for payment. You want to avoid bacteria from frequently-handled money transferring to the food. Instead, seek out two-person stalls where possible.

A sausage vendor grilling meat in Northern Thailand.

In addition, finding a street vendor who separates out potentially unsanitary food combinations is important. If there is raw meat or seafood to be cooked, is it kept away from the tortilla that will eventually house it? Try to avoid the stalls where raw materials are touching the ingredients that will be used for the final product.

Consider the cleanliness of the food stall or restaurant. When selecting a place, how are the dishes being washed? Is dirty water being used to rinse out the bowls and cutlery? You can avoid some of this by bringing your own chopsticks, but ultimately you might still fall ill. Watching how the restaurant cleans the dishes is an important step.

Mark Lowerson, an expat writer in Vietnam notes:

> For those with sensitive stomachs, and in the rare exceptional circumstances where something truly nasty may be lurking, it pays to be fairly vigilant. To guard against the risk of contracting stomach bugs, a few simple pointers are worth considering. Use of gloves and tongs is a pretty good sign that the vendor has a degree of awareness of food handling practices. A vendor who is well-groomed and scrupulously clean gets points, too. Look around the stall for clean glasses, crockery and chopsticks, tables and condiment vessels that are wiped clean. The fewer smears and fingerprints, the better. Carry a pad of hand wipes to clean your hands and chopsticks before you eat.
>
> Or, in Vietnam, do as the locals do – ineffectually rub each stick and your spoon with a dry paper napkin. In reality this action cannot be doing anything remotely cleansing but it will help you to fit in and feel like a local![22]

In cities such as Bangkok and Singapore, many vendors are marked with letters after inspection by the health ministry. An "A" grade for cleanliness in a Thai food court is a good place to start your food hunt.

Align your eating to when the locals eat their big meals. Is lunch the big protein meal of the day, with dinner a smaller option? Following the customary patterns of eating ensures that you follow the natural flow of food in the country. This includes power outages – if refrigeration and/or power is not consistent, you are best eating your meat earlier in the day. Buffet-style eating is especially troublesome if consuming outside these busier hours since food will be picked-over and also sitting in the heat post-meal time. I try to time my meals to just before the stalls get busy, eating an early lunch and an early dinner to ensure my pick of the freshest foods.

Tips for Eating in Africa

Writer Phil Paoletta of philintheblank.net is a long-time traveler to Africa, and has some advice for maximizing local eats while avoiding food-borne sickness:

- Many travelers avoid hibiscus juice/tea *(bissap)* because it's been made with local water. But *bissap* is boiled with sugar and the hibiscus flowers before it is later chilled.

- Rice dishes that are accompanied by a sauce that is served hot are usually your safest bets. These are often slow cooked and they are unlikely to make you ill.

- As far as when to eat, I would eat close to "normal" meal times for your destination: breakfast from 6: 00 a.m. – 8:30 a.m.; lunch from noon – 1:30 p.m.; dinner from 7:00 p.m. – 8:30 p.m. If you're getting lunch mid-afternoon, you will have limited eating options and what you do find will probably be lukewarm and not necessarily good for your intestinal tract!

- Most places have their own cutlery, but a few places don't have any and customers eat with their hands. *Soukouya* shops are one example: *soukouya* is slow cooked meat, beef or sheep, topped with fresh cut onions, rock salt and a bit of mustard and chili on the side. At those places, water basins and soap are always provided; just make sure you dry your hands well before you start eating.

- I find most of my eating spots through recommendations from friends, asking people on Twitter and Facebook, and also attending Couchsurfing group meet ups for particular cities. Worst case: I often just wander and ask around, looking for the most popular places.

Food should be hot and fully cooked through. This is extremely important, especially where you are worried about the food or sanitation. Preference should be given to street stalls or markets that make their own dish in front of you; you can see the freshly sourced ingredients used, and know how (and with what) it was prepared. When stalls have food that has been sitting out for hours, such as curries in pots that were prepared earlier in the day, use caution if the sanitation and/or refrigeration in the area are a concern. If you bite into a piece of your meal and it is tepid, it is safer to ask for a cooked-through version or choose another dish.

As with sourcing the food, the older the person recommending the food, the better. If the lineup for the street stall is full of families and older locals, that is the meal you typically want – they are the group with the most discerning tastes.

Bring your own chopsticks. Ensuring your cutlery is clean might get you some strange looks from locals, but your stomach will thank you.

Pay attention to water and ice. Water is a double-edged sword. In countries where filtered water is widely available, drinking frozen drinks or eating the local ice cream is safer than you would expect. However, iced drinks are where you want to be careful; too many backpackers have found a roadside smoothie unsettled their stomachs. Asking around if the water is filtered is a good start; your guesthouse or landlord is where you might want to begin this questioning process. In Thailand, for example, filtered water is available at low, subsidized costs and thus the ice is frozen from the safe water. However, in countries where filtered water is not widely available, it is best to avoid street smoothies and ice cream when you are not sure of how the water was sourced. Can I Drink the Water (canidrinkthewater.org) is a resource that can help ascertain when it is safe to imbibe.

Don't turn your back on dairy products. Note that some countries print a "manufactured on" date instead of a "best before date" on their dairy products. Yoghurt is valuable to replenish the 'good' bacteria like acidophilus (unless you are me and picked the wrong shop to buy it from). I try to eat pasteurized yoghurt at least once a day when on the road, aiming to keep good bacteria in my intestines.[23]

Quirky spice and perfume shop in Chefchaouen, Morocco.

Safe Eating in India

I asked Cameron Stauch to provide some tips for safe eating in a country many fear for food-borne illnesses:

The experience of eating street food in India can be immensely rewarding. But whether it is simply sipping a warming cup of chai or digging into a bowl of spiced stewed chickpeas with deep fried puffed up bread, I like to follow two simple rules:

- Follow the crowds: A busy stall with many patrons may indicate that the food is tasty and fresh, and with the high turnover there is less chance of food hanging around in unsanitary conditions. Likewise, a mixed crowd that includes children, women and well-groomed men, as opposed to a group of rickshawallahs, is another indication of a food stall with a decent reputation.

- Become a temporary vegetarian: The variety of vegetarian street snacks is plentiful and extremely delicious. Meat handling and storage practices in India are varied and constant refrigeration is not certain. While there are no guarantees, by limiting your meat consumption you can reduce your chances of experiencing the famous "Delhi belly".

Fruit and vegetable selection should be diligent as well. In countries where the water is safe, most raw fruit washed and then dried vigorously will be safe to eat. In places where the water cannot be consumed, fruit that does not have a thick skin or cannot be peeled should be avoided. Porous produce like lettuce and strawberries can also be an issue as contaminated water sinks into the fruit as it is still growing. As with traveling for the seasons, it is worth figuring out what fruits are in season so you can ensure that you are eating the freshest of what's available.

Mangosteens, one of my favorite snacks in Southeast Asia. They taste like a peach crossed with a lychee.

For travel with children, Christine Gilbert suggests carrying dried fruit and peelable fresh fruit. "In areas with questionable water, we avoid pre-cut fruit (sometimes they wash it with local untreated water) and look for whole fruits that we cut ourselves (especially fruit with a thick skin, which you can peel away and avoid pesticides or local bugs). We also bring some sweets, crackers or other packaged goods that last for quite a while. Dried fruit is really great, and, of course, lots of bottled water. Our son always surprises us though: he's been known to scarf down Indian curry and grilled chicken hearts with equal zeal."

Sometimes it's luck. As my yoghurt story indicates, you can be as diligent as possible and still get foiled somewhere along the way. Though I have fallen ill in North America more than abroad, I still do eat out at home. Conversely, despite my llama empanada incident, I still try to consume street food as much as possible. Relying on pure luck is not going to keep you healthy, but using the guidelines above will make your risk more calculated, and provide you with many memories of food and entertainment from your time abroad.

What If You Fall Ill?

If you get food poisoning or a stomach illness, then a visit to a local doctor might be in order. Many of them are familiar with traveler's diarrhea but also with any lingering viruses that are circulating in the region. I would caution against trying to rehydrate immediately with sweetened sport electrolyte drinks because I've found the high levels of sugar in those drinks actually make me feel worse if the bacteria is still in my system. Instead, I stick to a steady diet of oral rehydration salts, rice (bread is a substitute if you are not gluten-intolerant) and bananas. Hydrate as much as possible with plain water.

If you do get sick, consulting with your travel medical insurance provider is recommended to determine how much of your treatment they will cover. Your home doctor can be a comforting resource as well if you are concerned about the forms of treatment you are receiving abroad.

As a solo traveler, the times I've been sick are the times that have been the loneliest. It is not fun to have a stomach bug at home, let alone in a faraway place. However, the beauty of technology is that it can offer comfort from afar; I take advantage of Skype and Google Talk to reach out to family or friends at home. A few words of commiseration go a long way to making me feel better.

Jodi Ettenberg

Jodi Ettenberg

When I first began the process of writing this book, I struggled to frame my own passion for food and travel in a compelling way. I wanted to convey my excitement for low-cost food and urge everyone to use those cheap meals as their tool for learning as they traveled.

But when I started preliminary research for what would become *The Food Traveler's Handbook*, a theme began to emerge: people wanted to try local food, but they were worried about how to eat it safely.

Bit by bit this book morphed from a book about finding cheap eats to one that also addressed the desire to see the world through its food while coping with a fear of parasites and food illnesses. With several years of travel under my belt, I had lost sight of the initial wide-eyed terror I had felt when I first set out in 2008, not knowing what to eat, and not realizing that there were simple tricks that could help me do so safely.

Getting over my own reservations about food took an ambitious trial and error strategy, often yielding questionable results. Twinned with all the tasting was a dedication to understanding why people ate what they did. And as I started to learn through food, I developed a desire to dig deeper and to discover how food systems impacted the culture, history and politics of many of the countries I visited.

In this handbook, I wanted to paint a thorough portrait of the possibilities that lie in store if you focus on food as you travel, while also assuaging fear by sharing lessons that I learned the hard way. The book is not meant to replace your guidebooks or history books but to supplement them with on-the-ground practical knowledge that demystifies one of the main pillars of travel.

I encourage you to challenge your fears, to travel and discover through food.

A whole world of delicious meals and remarkable experiences awaits. Go ahead. Take your first bite.

Jodi Ettenberg

RESOURCES

Eating the Seasons

For **North America and the UK/Ireland**, use Eat the Seasons to see what fruit and vegetables are available at a given time of year: eattheseasons.com or eattheseasons.co.uk

Epicurious has handy visual guides for

Latin American produce:
epicurious.com/articlesguides/seasonalcooking/farmtotable/visualguidelatinamericanproduce

and **Asian produce:**
epicurious.com/articlesguides/seasonalcooking/farmtotable/visualguideasianproduce

Food options can be researched on the thorough Travel Independent country pages, which include **foods for each country:** travelindependent.info/countries.htm

Travel + Leisure has a helpful slideshow on **traveling in shoulder season** as well: travelandleisure.com/slideshows/shoulder-season-travel-secrets

Food Etiquette

International Dining Etiquette, divided by country:
etiquettescholar.com/dining_etiquette/international_dining_etiquette.html

A guide to **using chopsticks** for those starting out:
etiquettescholar.com/dining_etiquette/table_manners/utensil_etiquette.html#chopsticks

Wikipedia's thorough **chopstick etiquette** page:
en.wikipedia.org/wiki/Chopstick#Etiquette

Chinese dining etiquette:
en.wikipedia.org/wiki/Customs_and_etiquette_in_Chinese_dining

Japanese dining etiquette:
en.wikipedia.org/wiki/Japanese_cuisine#Dining_etiquette

Indian dining etiquette:
en.wikipedia.org/wiki/Etiquette_of_Indian_dining

Korean dining etiquette:
en.wikipedia.org/wiki/Korean_cuisine#Etiquette

Gestures from around the world:
globalbusinessleadership.com/gestures_mid_af.asp

General Customs

Cultural etiquette around the world from eDiplomat:
ediplomat.com/np/cultural_etiquette/cultural_etiquette.htm

Business etiquette and culture around the world:
cyborlink.com/default.htm

International tipping:
etiquettescholar.com/dining_etiquette/restaurant_etiquette/international_
tipping_guidelines.html

Etiquette in Latin America:
en.wikipedia.org/wiki/Etiquette_in_Latin_America

Kwintessential's **country custom guides:**
kwintessential.co.uk/resources/country-profiles.html

For women, Journeywoman's "What should I wear there" guide compiles **advice from other female travelers,** sorted by destination: journeywoman.com/ccc

Hand gestures you want to avoid (or get right!) as you travel: theatlantic.com/international/archive/2011/09/the-worlds-rudest-hand-gestures/245238

Packing Tips and Checklists

My **full first aid kit and packing lists** are here: legalnomads.com/wds

Gadling lists its top items to include in a **travel kit:** gadling.com/2010/12/21/top-fifteen-items-to-have-in-your-travel-first-aid-kit

The Adventure Doc's **vaccination page** describing each vaccine: adventuredocclinic.com/vaccines.html

The Centers for Disease Control and Prevention website includes **Traveler's Health recommendations:** cdc.gov/travel

The Public Health Agency of Canada has a travel health page for **immunizations and diseases** like dengue or malaria: phac-aspc.gc.ca/tmp-pmv/index-eng.php

Foreign Affairs and International Trade Canada country reports include **health information sorted by country:** voyage.gc.ca/countries_pays/menu-eng.asp

The World Health Organization's country-specific reports, each with an **immunization profile:** who.int/countries/en

Sick on the Road's **crash course to travel vaccinations:**
sickontheroad.com/2011/08/01/travel-immunizations-what-you-need-to-know

The Point-It Dictionary:
graf-editions.de/pointit/point_it_eng.html

Food safety preparation: a thorough and educational read pre-trip is the practical *How to Shit Around the World*, by Dr. Jane Wilson-Howarth and Kathleen Meyer.

Additional Packing Resources

For women:
answeringoliver.com/2012/02/my-rtw-packing-list.html and alittleadrift.com/rtw-travel/#pack

For men:
gqtrippin.com/rtw/his-rtw-packing-list and wanderingearl.com/how-does-a-permanent-nomad-pack

For couples:
getupandglobe.com/skott-and-shawnas-rtw-packing-lists

General site for travel and packing tips:
travelite.org

Insurance Information

IMG: imglobal.com
World Nomads: worldnomads.com
TravelGuard: travelguard.com
Clements Worldwide for electronics/possessions: clements.com
Handy **insurance chart to compare plans:** bootsnall.com/travel-insurance/travel-medical-insurance.html

Visa Information

For American citizens: travel.state.gov/travel/travel_1744.html
For Canadian Citizens: voyage.gc.ca/index-eng.asp
For Australian Citizens: dfat.gov.au/visas/index.html
For UK Citizens: fco.gov.uk/en/travel-and-living-abroad/passports1/entry-requirements
Generally: delta.com/planning_reservations/plan_flight/international_travel_information/visa_passport_information

Food Books to Whet your Appetite for Travel

* *Heat: An Amateur's Adventures as Kitchen Slave, Line Cook, Pasta-Maker, and Apprentice to a Dante-Quoting Butcher in Tuscany*, by Bill Buford
* *Edible History of Humanity*, by Tom Standage
* *The Physiology of Taste*, by Jean-Anthelme Brillat-Savarin
* *The Devil's Cup: A History of the World According to Coffee*, by Stewart Lee Allen
* *Shark's Fin and Sichuan Pepper: A Sweet-Sour Memoir of Eating in China*, by Fuchsia Dunlop
* *Spice: The History of a Temptation*, by Jack Turner Curry: A Biography
* *Eating Thai Food Guide: All-Inclusive Guide to Eating Thai Food*, by Mark Wiens (eatingthaifood.com)
* *The Omnivore's Dilemma: A Natural History in Four Meals*, by Michael Pollan
* *An Economist Gets Lunch: New Rules for Everyday Foodies*, by Tyler Cowen
* *Salt: A World History*, by Mark Kurlansky
* *Cod: The Biography of the Fish that Changed the World*, by Mark Kurlansky
* *The Encyclopedia of Herbs, Spices & Flavorings*, by Elisabeth Lambert Ortiz
* *The Story of Sushi: An Unlikely Saga of Raw Fish and Rice*, by Trevor Corson
* *1493: Uncovering the New World Columbus Created*, by Charles C. Mann
* *How the Potato Changed the World*, by Charles C. Mann smithsonianmag.com/history-archaeology/How-the-Potato-Changed-the-World.html?c=y&story=fullstory

- *The Fish That Ate the Whale: The Life and Times of America's Banana King*, by Rich Cohen
- *Food in History*, by Reay Tannahill
- *The Secret Life of Lobsters: How Fishermen and Scientists Are Unraveling the Mysteries of Our Favorite Crustacean*, by Trevor Corson
- *Empires of Food: Feast, Famine, and the Rise and Fall of Civilizations*, by Evan D.G. Fraser and Andrew Rimas
- *Hot Sour Salty Sweet: A Culinary Journey Through Southeast Asia*, by Naomi Duguid and Jeffrey Alford
- *The Mediterranean in the Ancient World*, by Fernand Braudel
- *Honey from a Weed: Fasting and Feasting in Tuscany, Catalonia, the Cyclades and Apulia*, by Patience Gray
- *The New Book of Middle Eastern Food*, by Claudia Roden
- *Arabesque: A Taste of Morocco, Turkey, and Lebanon*, by Claudia Roden
- *The Old World Kitchen: The Rich Tradition of European Peasant Cooking*, by Elisabeth Luard
- *Food: A Culinary History from Antiquity to the Present* by Jean-Louis Flandrin, Massimo Montanari and Albert Sonnenfeld
- *The Fortune Cookie Chronicles: Adventures in the World of Chinese Food*, by Jennifer 8. Lee
- *On Food and Cooking: The Science and Lore of the Kitchen*, by Harold McGee
- *The Food of China*, by N.E. Anderson
- *The Food of Paradise: Exploring Hawaii's Culinary Heritage*, by Rachel Laudan
- *The United States of Arugula: The Sun Dried, Cold Pressed, Dark Roasted, Extra Virgin Story of the American Food Revolution*, by David Kamp
- *Pure Ketchup: A History of America's National Condiment*, by Andrew F. Smith
- *The Food Chronology: A Food Lover's Compendium of Events and Anecdotes*, from Prehistory to Present, by James Trager
- *A Mediterranean Feast*, by Clifford Wright
- *A Moveable Feast: Life-Changing Food Adventures Around the World*, edited by Don George
- *Eating India: An Odyssey into the Food and Culture of the Land of Spices*, by Chitrita Banerji

- *World's Best Street Food*, by Lonely Planet
- *What I Eat: Around the World in 80 Diets*, by Peter Menzel and Faith D'Aluisio

Food Sites to Learn From

Edible Geography: ediblegeography.com
Food Politics: foodpolitics.com
Gastronomica: gastronomica.org
Gernot Katzer's Spice Page: uni-graz.at/~katzer/engl/index.html
Grist Food: grist.org/food
Legal Nomads Food Resources Page: legalnomads.com/food-book
Patak's Love of Curry Spice Page: pataks.co.uk/love-of-curry/spice-guide. aspx
Politics of the Plate: politicsoftheplate.com
Smithsonian Magazine's Food and Think Blog: blogs.smithsonianmag. com/food
The Cook's Thesaurus: foodsubs.com
Zester Daily: zesterdaily.com/Travel

Food Sites to Drool Over

Chowhound (Extremely food-obsessed users with trip reports from countries around the world, suggestions about where to eat and many options for street eats): chowhound.chow.com/boards

CNNGo's Food (Focus on Asia and Australia with food how-to's and mini guides for finding the best eats): cnngo.com/eat

Culinary Back Streets (Food in Shanghai, Istanbul and Athens, by the founders of Istanbul Eats): culinarybackstreets.com

Eating Asia (Istanbul and Southeast Asia focus, emphasis on cultural and local aspect of food from writer Robyn Eckhardt and her husband Dave Hagerman who is a photographer): eatingasia.typepad.com

Food by Country (exactly what it sounds like): foodbycountry.com

Global Table Adventure (Worldwide): globaltableadventure.com

Gluten-free Girl (Recipes, narrative and photography about gluten-free eats): glutenfreegirl.com

James Beard Bites (James Beard culinary award blog, featuring politics, food trends and food news): jamesbeard.org/blog

MidEats (Middle Eastern food and culture): mideats.com

Migrationology (Asia focus, emphasis on food photo essays and street food guides in different cities around the world): migrationology.com

Naomi Duguid (James Beard award-winning author with a philosophy of immersion through food and musings about culture and eating): naomiduguid.blogspot.ca

Smitten Kitchen (Fearless cooking from a tiny kitchen in NYC; great photography): smittenkitchen.com

Tasting Cultures (Worldwide): tastingcultures.blogspot.ca

Taxi Gourmet (Eating the world via recommendations from taxi drivers. Mainly in New York, Buenos Aires and Berlin): taxigourmet.com

The Perennial Plate (Adventurous and sustainable eating, primarily video): theperennialplate.com

Umami Mart (International food and drink blog with focus on Japanese cuisine): umamimart.com

Viet World Kitchen (Asian recipes and articles from cooking teacher and writer Andrea Nguyen): vietworldkitchen.com

Endnotes

[1] See Raven Hanna's "Feynman's Flower" blog for more, specifically Touched by Molecules, madewithmolecules.com/blog/?tag=uc-berkeley, (October 9, 2008). In addition, a Nature Neuroscience article on Sichuan peppercorn provides further insight into the science behind the sensation. Diana Bautista, Yaron Sigal, Aaron Milstein, Jennifer Garrison, Julie Zorn, Pamela Tsuruda, Roger Nicoll & David Julius, Pungent agents from Szechuan peppers excite sensory neurons by inhibiting two-pore potassium channels, Nature Neuroscience 11, 772 – 779, nature.com/neuro/journal/v11/n7/abs/nn.2143.html, (2008).

[2] Dan Jurafsky, The Cosmopolitan Condiment: An Exploration of Ketchup's Chinese Origins, slate.com/articles/life/food/2012/05/ketchup_s_chinese_origins_how_it_evolved_from_fish_sauce_to_today_s_tomato_condiment.single.html, (2012).

[3] Jim Yardley, 100 Days of Madness as the 'King of Fruits' Is Celebrated Again, New York Times, nytimes.com/2012/06/04/world/asia/mango-season-has-india-in-thrall.html?_r=2&pagewanted=all, (June 4, 2012).

[4] See, example, a photo taken by Paula Bronstein after the tsunami in Japan. Japan Earthquake: Two Weeks Later, theatlantic.com/infocus/2011/03/japan-earthquake-two-weeks-later/100034/#img26, (March 25, 2011).

[5] The Mendeleyev Journal, Meal Traditions and Etiquette, russianreport. wordpress.com/russian-cuisine-main-salads-soups-desserts/meal-traditions-and-etiquette.

[6] Etiquette in North America, Wikipedia.org, en.wikipedia.org/wiki/Etiquette_in_North_America.

[7] Travellers' and Tourists' Health Advisory Clinic, redcross.or.th/old/english/service/medical_travel.php.

[8]Food and Agriculture Organization of the United Nations, Fermented Fruits and Vegetables: a Global Perspective, fao.org/docrep/x0560e/x0560e06. htm#1.3.1, (1998).

[9]For more breakfast ideas: 50 of the World's Best Breakfasts,blog. hostelbookers.com/travel/best-breakfast/, (July 20, 2012).

[10]See Layne Mosler's Taxi Gourmet site at taxigourmet.com for the taxi-as-food-source theory in action.

[11]For a great piece about communal baking see Annia Ciezadlo's Bread of Beirut, Granta Magazine, granta.com/New-Writing/Bread-of-Beirut, (August 2, 2012).

[12]For cooking class suggestions, see Lina Goldberg's 10 International Cooking Classes on CNNGo, cnngo.com/explorations/eat/10-incredible-international-cooking-classes-465955, (May 16, 2012).

[13]Tyler Cowen, An Economist Gets Lunch, at page 72, (2012).

[14]For more street food suggestions in Bangkok, see Mark Wiens, Top 16 Bangkok Food Sanctuaries, migrationology.com/2011/05/top-16-bangkok-street-food-sanctuaries/, (2011).

[15]For more, see Hanoi Street Food Guide, Savour Asia, savourasia.com/content/view/5/10 (2009).

[16]For Hong Kong food suggestions see Christopher DeWolf, Izzy Ozawa, Tiffany Lam, Virginia Lau, and Zoe Li's 40 Hong Kong Foods We Can't Live Without, CNNGo.com, cnngo.com/hong-kong/none/40-things-eat-hong-kong-coronary-arrest-820489, (July 13, 2010).

[17]Paul Theroux, Paul Theroux's Quest to Define Hawaii, Smithsonian Magazine, smithsonianmag.com/travel/Paul-Therouxs-Quest-to-Define-Hawaii.html, (May 2012).

[18]The UN checklists are also available online. UNEP World Conservation Monitoring Centre, Checklist of CITES Species, cites.org/eng/resources/pub/checklist11/CITES_species_index.pdf (2011).

[19]Full report available online. The Pew Charitable Trusts Environmental Group, Navigating Global Shark Conservation: Current Measures and Gaps, pewenvironment.org/uploadedFiles/PEG/Publications/Report/Navigating%20Global%20Shark%20Conservation_Current%20Measures%20and%20Gaps%207%206%2012.pdf (2012).

[20]Centers for Disease Control and Prevention, Travelers' Diarrhea, cdc.gov/ncidod/dbmd/diseaseinfo/travelersdiarrhea_g.htm#prevent.

[21]For food borne illness reports in America, see The Barf Blog, barfblog. foodsafety.ksu.edu/barfblog.

[22]Mark Lowerson, Street Food Safety, Travelfish, travelfish.org/feature/235 (April 18, 2012).

[23]More about good bacteria from the New York Times: Gina Kolata, In Good Health? Thank Your 100 Trillion Bacteria, nytimes.com/2012/06/14/health/human-microbiome-project-decodes-our-100-trillion-good-bacteria.html, (June 13, 2012).

Jodi Ettenberg

Jodi Ettenberg was born in Montreal and has been eating her way around the world since April 2008. In addition to publishing *Legal Nomads (legalnomads. com)*, which chronicles her ongoing travels, meals and transportation misadventures, Jodi is a contributing editor for *Longreads* and a freelance writer and photographer for *The Hipmunk* and *G Adventures*. Prior to founding *Legal Nomads*, Jodi worked as a corporate lawyer in New York City. She frequently speaks about social media strategy, food and travel, and curation. She gets the shakes when she goes too long without eating sticky rice.

Jodi Ettenberg

Jodi Ettenberg

CPSIA information can be obtained
at www.ICGtesting.com
Printed in the USA
LVIW011051241212
313092LV00001B